Quick Color Tab Reference for Butterfly Groups

The Guide to
Butterflies

of *Oregon* and
Washington

By William Neill
Photography by Doug Hepburn and William Neill

WESTCLIFFE PUBLISHERS

www.westcliffepublishers.com

International Standard Book Number: 1-56579-392-7

Editor: Kelly Kordes Anton
Designer: Carol Pando
Production Manager: Craig Keyzer

Published by:
Westcliffe Publishers, Inc.
P.O. Box 1261
Englewood, CO 80150
www.westcliffepublishers.com

Printed in Hong Kong by Midas Printing

Library of Congress Cataloging-in-Publication Data:

Neill, William, 1929-
    The guide to butterflies of Oregon and Washington / by William Neill ; photography by
    Doug Hepburn and William Neill.
      p. cm.
    Includes bibliographical references (p.).
    ISBN 1-56579-392-7
      1. Butterflies--Washington (State)--Identification. 2.
    Butterflies--Oregon--Identification. I. Hepburn, Douglas J. II. Title.

QL551.W2 N45 2001
595.78'9'09795--dc21
                                             2001022519

Please Note: The author has made every attempt to correctly identify the butterflies in the
region, their host plants, and their habitats. When exploring butterfly habitats, risk is always
a factor, especially in backcountry and high-mountain travel. Many of the areas described in
this book can be dangerous, especially when weather is adverse or unpredictable, and when
unforeseen events or conditions create a hazardous situation. It is the responsibility of the users
of this guide to learn the necessary skills for safe backcountry travel, and to exercise caution in
potentially hazardous areas, especially on glaciers and avalanche-prone terrain. The author
and publisher disclaim any liability for injury or other damage caused by backcountry traveling
or performing any other activity described in this book.

*For more information about other fine books and calendars from Westcliffe Publishers, please
contact your local bookstore, call us at 1-800-523-3692, write for our free color catalog, or
visit us on the Web at* **www.westcliffepublishers.com**.

First Frontispiece: *Montane meadow in the Goat Wilderness, Washington, with Mount
Adams in the distance. Photo by Charles Gurche.*
Title Page: *Two-tailed Swallowtail. Photo by Doug Hepburn.*
Opposite: *A mating pair of Silvery Blues. Photo by Doug Hepburn.*

Acknowledgments

Let me take this opportunity to name some people who helped make this book happen.

First, my father, James Maffett Neill, who got me interested in science. Second, there's my mother, Jessie, who allowed the insect zoo to spill from its cardboard box and into my bedroom from 1940 on.

My wife, Sara, and our children—Jim, Bill, and Valerie—initially joined me in my rambles through the countryside, then later they led me and inspired me with their own interests in the outdoors.

Among the people I'm indebted to for sharing their field experiences and for their influence on my understanding of butterflies are: Ray Albright, Ernst Dornfeld, Dave Faulkner, Paul Grey, Paul Hammond, John Hinchliff, Warren Kiel, Dave McCorkle, Bill McGuire, Bob Pyle, Harold Rice, Bob Robbins, Ken Smith, Ray Stanford, Ernest Williams, and Dave Winters. Dave McCorkle reviewed the text for accuracy and suggested helpful changes.

Finally, thanks to my son, Bill, for his work in coaxing the book into a readable shape and to Westcliffe Publishers for producing it in palpable form.

Swallowtails congregate at a wet spot on an old dirt road. Photo by William Neill.

Foreword

In the 30 years that I have known Bill Neill, I have come to respect his ability to bring a sense of curiosity to his observations of butterflies, as well as to arrive at thoughtful insights about their behavior. In *The Guide to Butterflies of Oregon and Washington*, I find the musings Bill shares quite stimulating—even inspirational—as he takes us to his favorite meadows and woodlands to find these magnificent creatures. While reading a particular passage in this engaging book, I said to myself, "I've been to that meadow! How did I miss feeling that sense of awe at those Checkerspots sipping nectar from the dogbane blossoms spotlighted by sunbeams?"

Through his well-trained eyes, Bill provides a spirited look at 100 butterflies of the Pacific Northwest. This book especially meets the needs of amateur naturalists who are interested in learning about the region's butterflies. Bill teaches us how to identify our local butterflies and how to watch what they are doing in order to understand them better. But the greatest value of this book may be its ability to motivate readers to become more personally involved with the natural world around them.

David V. McCorkle
Professor of Biology, emeritus
Western Oregon University, Monmouth, Oregon

An Edith's Checkerspot drinks sweat from a child's hand. Photo by William Neill.

Contents

Cow parsnip covering a cliff above Sisters Rocks in Curry County, Oregon. Photo by Steve Terrill.

How To Use This Guide

The front part of this book contains scientific information on butterflies, useful tips on locating and observing butterflies on your own, and a description of the types of terrain in Oregon and Washington. A Species List of 100 local butterfly species precedes individual descriptions of the butterflies. The butterflies are organized into 15 groups, and colored tabs on the pages allow for easy reference to these groups (see page 1). The back of the book gives advice on creating your own butterfly garden and nursery, a glossary of terms used in the book, a bibliography and recommended reading, and an index.

LOOKING AT THE PICTURES

You can use this book simply as a field guide to help you identify the butterflies you see in Oregon, Washington, and elsewhere in the Pacific Northwest. Skip the daunting blocks of text and begin instead with the color photographs. You'll see butterflies just as you'll encounter them in the field. We not only tried to vary the picture content, illustrating butterflies engaged in different kinds of activities, but we selected poses that reveal the important field marks that distinguish one butterfly from another. To preserve a natural look, we relied on ambient sunlight (no artificial flash) to illuminate the butterflies and their surroundings.

All the butterflies pictured live in Oregon and/or Washington. With this book there's no wading through pictures of other butterflies, which complicates the use of field guides that cover broad geographic ranges. Other photos in the book show some of the different butterfly habitats found in these two states.

READING THE TEXT

Sooner or later your curiosity (or guilt) will get you back to try the introductory text, where you know you should have started in the first place. Then, you'll learn how to get the most out of watching butterflies in the field. You'll discover how butterflies see, hear, smell, and touch the things around them; how their lives have been linked with plants through the ages; and how their amazing life cycles are purposefully integrated with seasons of the year. In our description of each species, we list the host plant to help you in identifying eggs, caterpillars, and butterflies.

Butterflies are much more than beautiful objects. Butterflies are animals that take action when they get hungry, tired, or cold. Their lives are driven by a will to reproduce and to have their own offspring succeed in a competitive, perilous world.

With the background information entrenched in your mind, turn back to the photographs and venture out to the field. You'll be able to see much more of what is there!

UNDERSTANDING DESCRIPTIVE TERMS ▰▰

In the Species Descriptions section of this book, starting on page 49, we offer a representative photograph of each species along with the butterfly's common name, size, habitat, and more. Review this diagram to familiarize yourself with the anatomy of a butterfly's wing before reading the descriptions. Other terms used in the book can be found in the glossary on page 154.

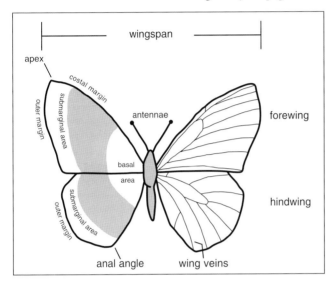

The Species Descriptions are presented as follows:

- **Name:** Common name (alternative common name).

- *Name:* Scientific name (alternative scientific name).

- **Wingspan:** Distance between the tips of the forewings when positioned as shown in the diagram above.

- **Description:** Field marks and other significant physical features of the species. Wing fringes are hairs at the outer margins of wings. See the diagram above for definitions of all wing areas.

- **Range:** The butterfly's geographic distribution within Oregon and Washington, based on recorded lepidopterists' field observations compiled by John Hinchliff in *The Distribution of the Butterflies of Oregon* and *The Distribution of the Butterflies of Washington* (both published by Oregon State University, 1994 and 1996, respectively).

- **Habitat:** Type of environment where the species is typically found.

- **Host plant:** Plant or plants most frequently used by the species' caterpillar.

A brief description of the butterfly follows this introductory information.

Snowberry Checkerspot. Photo by William Neill.

TAKING THE PHOTOGRAPHS

Taking pictures of butterflies is no easy feat. You're working toward a small and moving target in varying conditions. We did our best to capture a representative of each species. The equipment we used and the objectives we applied in selecting photographs for publication were as follows:

Equipment

We took the butterfly photographs with an Olympus Pen F half-frame camera mounted with a 100-200mm f5.6 zoom lens and bellows, or an Olympus OM-1 camera mounted with a 75-150mm f4 zoom lens and either one or two 2.5 cm extenders. These are compact, lightweight setups, suitable for pursuing a mobile target. Kodachrome ASA 25 or 64 film was employed for every picture. We depended exclusively on natural sunlight. Without flash lighting, the fine-grained slow film limited the workable exposure settings. Aperture f8 at 1/60 second was typical. Butterflies usually don't pose long for their portrait, so the camera was handheld, with an elbow braced against the ground or a knee for stability when possible. For pictures of eggs or pupae, we often used a tripod.

For the first two years of this project, Doug Hepburn took all the photographs. I watched, learned from his experience in nature photography, copied him, and later took photographs as well.

Objectives

When photographing butterflies and selecting pictures for publication, we considered three main objectives:

1. Field Identification. The picture must demonstrate the most important field marks that distinguish the butterfly from other species. In some cases this meant viewing the underside of the wings, in others the top of the wings.

2. Illustrate Behavior. We chose photographs that show how butterflies live their lives, illustrating topics discussed with words in the introductory text. The text explains, for example, that antennae are equipped with chemical receptors; the photograph on page 19 shows the antennae touching the flower to taste it while the butterfly probes for nectar. It's one thing to read that a butterfly basks in sunlight to warm its body; it's another thing to see the butterfly actually bending its knees to lower its body onto a warm rock.

3. Show Surroundings. To show butterflies in their natural surroundings, both needed to be visible. Ideally, the space around the butterfly is quietly discernible—showing itself as a lush meadow instead of desert gravel—but not so interesting that it competes for attention. A blurred, out-of-focus background that is distinctly but gently contrasted with the butterfly by color or degree of darkness aesthetically integrates the butterfly and its environment. In general, this effect is achieved most successfully with natural ambient lighting.

A female Sara's Orange Tip feeding on a blue anemone flower. Photo by William Neill.

Butterflies as Animals

To get started learning about butterflies, you need to understand the type of animal they are, how they reproduce, and their life cycles. Armed with this information, you'll have a clearer understanding of what to look for when you spot butterflies in the field.

BUTTERFLY CLASSIFICATION

The animal kingdom is dominated by two principal groups: vertebrates and arthropods. The soft body of vertebrate animals is slung from a rigid internal skeleton. The skeleton of arthropods is on the outside, like a shell. The hard external skeleton of arthropods provides protection and defines their shape, holding the soft parts in place. Ancestors of these two groups diverged when animals were at a primitive stage of development, and the fantastic array of species that now exists among vertebrates (all fish, amphibians, reptiles, birds, and mammals) and arthropods (all insects, spiders, and crustaceans) appears to be the outcome of branching and re-branching along two separate evolutionary paths.

Edith's Checkerspot. Photo by William Neill.

Besides their external skeleton (or exoskeleton), another characteristic of arthropods is their jointed legs. An arthropod with six jointed legs is an insect. Spiders, crabs, and centipedes are examples of arthropods with more than six legs. The adaptability of the insect model of life in fitting into the earth's environmental niches is certainly remarkable. More than one-half of all known animal species are insects.

Some insects have wings covered by scales; these are called lepidoptera (scaly-wings). Lepidoptera are separated into two groups: butterflies and moths. The most reliable feature that distinguishes them from each other is their antennae. The antennae terminate with knobs in butterflies; antennae of moths are pointed. Other, less reliable, differences include: the bodies of butterflies are usually more slender and less hairy; butterflies seldom fly at night; and butterflies usually rest with their wings held either horizontally or folded tightly together over their back, not "tented" over their body as with many moths.

Opposite: *Rhododendrons and Indian paintbrush drenched in early morning fog.*
Photo by Steve Terrill.

SPECIES AND VARIATION ▰▰▰▰▰▰

Animals that mate with each other and produce viable and fertile offspring are members of the same species. This is not the only definition of "species," but it's a useful one. What keeps the borders of a species intact? Members of a species generally don't mate with other species. They exchange and mix genetic material only with each other. You will see some variation in physical characteristics from one individual to the next within the breeding population of a species. The physical differences between different species are usually pronounced enough that even closely related species are recognizable from each other. Anglewings, Tortoiseshells, and Admirals are examples of butterflies in which each species has a relatively consistent appearance. For Fritillaries and Checkerspots, there is more variation within a given species, sometimes making it difficult to decide which species an individual butterfly should be assigned to.

Another type of variation occurs in some species—individuals in one geographic area look different from those in another. For example, the whole population of Mountain Fritillary in the Ochoco Mountains has shiny silver spots on the wings. Not so for Mountain Fritillaries on Steens Mountain, 100 miles to the south. There, the spots are dull yellow. This is a consistent finding: You'd never mistake a Steens Mountain Fritillary for one from the Ochocos.

Butterfly colonies that are isolated from each other by unsuitable intervening habitat lose the opportunity for interbreeding. Basically, butterflies don't fly that far. Over many generations, an isolated colony may evolve its own characteristics, including different spots. The two colonies inhabiting the Ochoco Mountains and Steens Mountain aren't really separate species, but they're recognizable from each other. The different colonies are then sometimes referred to as separate subspecies.

How unique must a colony be to earn the title of subspecies? After all, minor differences between local populations of a given species are a common, almost ubiquitous phenomenon. Should there be separate names for each one? That would be pretty complicated. There is more debate than consensus among the experts on the question of naming subspecies. The general point to keep in mind is that ordinary variability within a species occurs on the same piece of land. Subspecies require reproductive isolation, usually on a geographic basis.

The total range of most butterfly species is not extensive. The eastern and western edges of the United States each have their own separate species lists, with an overlap of only about 20 percent. Even within its overall geographic range, a species may be found only in isolated colonies, individuals only occasionally wandering into intervening, less suitable territory.

More than 10,000 known species of butterflies exist on Earth, approximately 800 of which occur in North America. Some 160 to 170 species have been found in the area encompassing Oregon and Washington. An energetic, experienced person might spot half that number in one year by undertaking multiple expeditions around these two states throughout the spring and summer. The other species are scarce, confined to a small area, or are occasional strays from their breeding bases in other states.

A Butterfly's Body

Anatomy

This Oregon Swallowtail is hardening its wings shortly after emerging from its pupa. The body has three main segments: head, thorax, and abdomen. Attached to the head are a pair of prominent, dark, protuberant eyes covered by numerous separate facets sensitive to light. The eyes are better at detecting motion than at forming a clear, focused image. They perceive color, even in the ultraviolet range, which is invisible to us. Two antennae stick out from the top of the head; these are equipped with receptors for touch and for identifying different chemical substances. The mouth of an adult butterfly is a flexible, hollow tube, which is kept coiled in a tight circle tucked under the head. Part of the coil is visible in this picture. The tube can be straightened and extended to reach nectar within flowers or to suck other liquid nutrients such as water or vegetable sap.

This Oregon Swallowtail is hardening its wings within an hour of emerging from the pupa, demonstrating the external anatomy of the adult butterfly. Photo by William Neill.

The thorax is the locomotive center, providing attachments for the four wings, six legs, and the muscles that move these appendages. Five of the six legs are showing here. The legs are long, slender, and jointed. This butterfly is in a hanging posture, the foot hooks providing a firm grip on the twig. Tiny muscles located within the thorax as well as within the legs themselves can flex or extend the joints.

We can see the underside of the wings, one entire hindwing, and the tip of a forewing. The wings are thin, but stiff enough to support the butterfly's weight when airborne. The wings are reinforced by struts, called veins, which are black in this swallowtail. Tiny, overlapping scales cover the wings in rows something like the shingles on the roof of a house. At this magnification, you can appreciate individual scales within the blue area of the hindwing where blue and black scales are mixed. The flight muscles are within the thorax and move the wings indirectly by distorting the thoracic exoskeleton to which the wings are fastened. The attachment of the wings to the body is delicate, allowing free movement in more than one plane.

The butterfly's abdomen houses the renal, digestive, and reproductive systems. This is a male, and his abdomen ends with a pair of triangular plates (or claspers), which he uses to grasp and help stabilize the female's abdomen during copulation.

The entire body is covered by fine yellow hairs. Underneath these hairs is the tough exoskeleton that encloses and protects the soft internal structures. The exoskeleton is made of a mesh of chitin fibers (chemically similar to wood, not bone) embedded in a protein matrix (like concrete reinforced by steel bars). The exoskeleton is rigid over the head and thorax, and more flexible over the abdomen.

Internal Fluid Circulation and Breathing

In butterflies, the internal organs are surrounded by fluid (hemolymph)—which functions somewhat like blood—through which they receive nutrients and hormones. The hemolymph circulates throughout the body, propelled by rhythmic contractions of a muscular vessel that runs through the abdomen and thorax. The hemolymph enters the tubular "heart" through openings near the heart's back (posterior) end. As the muscular tube contracts, valves within it direct the compressed hemolymph towards the head. The hemolymph squirts from the front (anterior) end of the tube, enters the free liquid space within the body, percolates past the living cells, and finally re-enters the posterior pores of the heart.

In insects, breathing is carried out completely independently from internal fluid circulation. A separate network of tubes carries fresh air directly to the cells, terminating in fine branches in all parts of the body. The opening to the outside is through a series of pores along the sides of the body, most of which are situated in the abdomen. Butterflies and caterpillars do not breathe through their mouth as we do, and they will drown if their abdomens are kept under water.

It's interesting to compare this breathing arrangement with our own. Vertebrates, including humans, evolved a single strategy for transporting both liquid and gas within the body. Blood is pumped by the heart through a network of closed tubes that branch into microscopic capillaries to reach the cells. The same blood passes through the lungs, where it comes into contact with fresh air, picking up oxygen and discarding carbon dioxide. This marvelously efficient design for rapid, distant transport has allowed the evolution of huge vertebrate animals, such as dinosaurs, elephants, and whales. Butterflies and other arthropods have settled on a design that serves them well, judging by their evolutionary success, but it is less capable of transporting air over long distances, thus limiting their possible size. Lobsters and horseshoe crabs are about the biggest arthropods I can think of.

Temperature Regulation

Insects are cold blooded—the temperature inside them varies according to the temperature around them. Butterfly muscles work best at about 80–100 degrees Fahrenheit. When it is cooler than that, butterflies move less quickly and are an easier target as potential meals. Therefore, butterflies keep out of sight when cold. The temperature in many climates is below 80 degrees much of the time, so butterflies wouldn't have much chance to be about conducting their business. To get around this problem, butterflies raise their body temperatures by absorbing radiant energy from the sun; this is called basking.

When basking, butterflies orient themselves to the sunshine in a manner that maximizes radiant heat absorption. The wings, with their large surface areas, act as heat collectors. Butterflies hold their wings in one of two positions: out flat to each side of the body in a horizontal plane (dorsal basking), or clasped together over the back (ventral basking). In either case, the surface of the wing facing the sun is held perpendicular to the sun's rays. Heat gathered by the wings is conducted to the thorax and muscles, where it counts. Dark surfaces absorb heat best. Alpine and subarctic varieties of butterflies, those with the greatest temperature challenge, tend to have fuzzier, darker bodies as well as darker coloring of the adjacent portions of their wings, which enhances heat absorption.

Butterflies often choose warm, cozy niches for basking—places with their own microclimate, such as sunny cups of foliage with still air or dark stones that have been in the sun for awhile. The benefit of basking is that the temperature of thoracic muscles can rise as much as 10–15 degrees Fahrenheit above the ambient temperature, often a crucial difference.

Once butterflies begin to fly, their working muscles contribute heat. To maintain the warm thoracic muscles while flying through cool air, butterflies depend on a balance of continued absorption of solar energy, muscle metabolism, and heat carried away from the surface of the body by moving air.

Pale Swallowtail on a columbine flower, east slope of the Cascade Mountains in Oregon.
Photo by William Neill.

REPRODUCTION ▰▰▰▰▰▰▰▰▰▰▰▰

Continuity of Life through DNA

Like other animals, bodies of butterflies wear out. The species continues because the mortal bodies are only temporary carriers of durable genes: complex DNA molecules that are the blueprint for a new body similar to the old one. DNA molecules are not passed on intact, however. An offspring receives DNA from both parents, in an ovum from its mother and in sperm from its father. Each ovum receives a different mixture of the mother's maternal and paternal DNA molecules. Likewise, each sperm receives a different mixture of the father's maternal and paternal DNA molecules. Moreover, the molecules themselves fragment and reassemble into new molecules as the ova and sperm are formed. Each offspring, therefore, is endowed with a unique set of DNA molecules and will be slightly different from its parents and siblings.

Of course, this molecular explanation of how butterflies make copies of themselves only happens if a male and female, two small animals out in all that space, find and recognize each other, and then physically join together to mate.

Finding a Mate

With butterflies the male takes the initiative. In some species, he charts a route and patrols it looking for a mate. The route might be a 100-meter path joining two meadows. Swallowtails, Whites, and Sulfurs employ patrolling as a mating tactic. Other butterflies, such as Anglewings, Admirals, Hairstreaks, and Skippers, more often locate females by perching. The male claims a vantage point—for example, a bush, or the relic of last autumn's aster still sticking up at the edge of the field—where he waits for a prospect to fly by. He darts from his perch to investigate practically anything that moves within his sight: another butterfly, a bird, or a person. If necessary, he defends his position by driving away any intruding rival male, sometimes chasing him skyward in a spiral path, then returning triumphantly to his original lookout.

When a male spots a female, the potential mates begin their courtship by sizing each other up visually. The two butterflies want to ensure that they are dealing with a member of their own species and that this candidate appears fit enough to contribute desirable genetic attributes to their shared offspring. Is the color right, are the ritual courting moves in order? Many species emit special chemicals called pheromones, which can be detected and assessed by the partner. If she is favorably impressed by these preliminaries, the female makes herself available. She may land on the ground where she can be approached by the male. He attempts to attach the tip of his abdomen to hers. She flutters off, perhaps is pursued, and alights again. She may cooperate in the copulation, or she may avert her abdomen and depart. As a final precaution against mistaken identity, many species possess unique genital structures that fit together in copulation like lock and key—but they don't fit with other species, even closely related ones.

Mating

During mating, the male injects a capsule containing millions of sperm (a spermatophore) into the exit pore of the oviduct located at the end of the female's abdomen. This spermatophore migrates up the oviduct to reach a side chamber, where it is stored. Copulation usually occurs soon after the female emerges from her pupa, at a time when the eggs in her ovaries are not yet mature. A few days later, mature eggs, singly or in bunches (depending on the species), descend the oviduct, where they pass the waiting sperm and are fertilized prior to their exit.

The male and female remain coupled for several minutes to an hour or longer. It's a perilous time, for they are not so agile in this predicament. They usually seek cover in vegetation, although they can fly and sometimes are seen traveling or feeding at flowers while attached.

Often, a female mates only once. A single spermatophore contains plenty of sperm to fertilize all her eggs. Not all females, however, confine themselves. Some may copulate again, perhaps because a subsequent suitor appears to offer preferable genes.

Parenting

Once he has contributed his spermatophore, the parental role of the male is completed. For the female, searching for the proper host plant and laying eggs dominate her activities for as long as she lives. She's meticulous about choosing locations that will give her offspring the best possible chance for survival. Will the sun exposure ensure warmth for the embryo's growth? Is the plant big enough to yield adequate foliage for the caterpillar? Is the quality of foliage healthy? Which position on the leaf will be most hidden from predators? This is her one chance to focus all her maternal instincts on the future welfare of her children. Once the egg leaves her body, the female departs the scene, and the new generation receives no further care from either parent.

Interaction between female and male is limited to the brief period of courtship and copulation. They make no attempt to forge the bond that is so important among mammals and birds, who share in the nurturing of their young over a long period of time. Limiting parental care frees up resources that are instead spent on producing a very large number of eggs. Only a small percentage of eggs need to survive to ensure a stable population.

Stages of Metamorphosis

a. Anise Swallowtail egg on desert parsley

b. young caterpillar, one or two weeks old

c. fully grown caterpillar, four or five weeks old

d. caterpillar preparing to form a pupa

e. fully developed pupa, the next day

f. same pupa, the following spring.

BUTTERFLY LIFE CYCLE ▰▰▰▰▰

Growth and Maturation (Metamorphosis)

The development of a butterfly, the transition from egg to full-size adult, proceeds through distinct phases, each with its own physical form. This process is known as metamorphosis, which is Greek for "change of form." This may seem like a tortuous path to adulthood, but as a strategy, metamorphosis has its advantages. Growing from a single cell to a complex adult organism is broken down into separate steps, assignments, and different physical configurations designed to carry out most effectively the assignment at hand.

Form 1: Egg

A butterfly egg is a little smaller than a pinhead. At the outset, it consists of the following three elements: a single microscopic cell empowered with the genetic blueprint for creating all the details of a marvelous butterfly, a relatively huge store of food (or yolk), and a tough shell that isolates the egg's contents from its surroundings. The shell is permeable enough for the living cells to breathe, while it prevents the egg from drying out.

The assignment during the egg stage is to transform the egg into a free-living organism capable of foraging on its own by the time the food provided within the egg is exhausted. The original single cell grows and divides repeatedly, using the stored food to form a mass of cells that is the beginning of an embryo. If we could witness this, we would see something vaguely resembling an animal form beginning to arise from the amorphous yolk material. In a matter of only a few days, a complex creature that can move about at will and perform purposeful actions is created and poised to step out and test its personality in the outside world. In the process of replicating a butterfly, surely the greatest step of all takes place as the embryo matures within the egg.

Form 2: Larva (Caterpillar)

The infant caterpillar, or mature embryo, chews its way through the eggshell and crawls out into the open. Its first meal is the remains of the empty eggshell. The caterpillar is equipped with mandibles for chewing leaves, a large digestive tract, and short legs permitting enough mobility to move from one foraging site to the next. The objective is to convert leaves into body mass. The caterpillar's growth is prodigious, amounting to more than a hundredfold increase in bulk within a period of a few weeks, all without significant change in form or function.

The caterpillar's exoskeleton is not very elastic and it must be replaced periodically to accommodate such rapid enlargement. To do this, the surface layer separates partially from an inner layer of actively multiplying cells. These cells form a new, larger exoskeleton underneath the old, the new layer temporarily wrinkled upon itself. At this point, the caterpillar expands by engulfing air, and the old exoskeleton splits away completely and is sloughed aside. The underlying layer is now free to unwrinkle and harden. The caterpillar immediately appears significantly larger, but the enlargement is mainly air. Subsequent growth of body tissue displaces the air. A caterpillar molts in this way four or five times, depending on the species.

Form 3: Pupa (Chrysalis)

Fully grown, the caterpillar finally stops eating and begins to wander. It locates a secluded place, and, in most species, attaches itself by silk strands to something rigid: a stiff stem, twig, or overhanging rock. The suspended caterpillar stops moving, sometimes ejects excess fluid, and shrinks. In two or three days, it sheds the outer covering to reveal a compact pupa. The pupa is motionless and has essentially no interaction with its surroundings. If provoked vigorously, it may respond by thrashing from side to side. The protoplasm amassed by the caterpillar is now broken down into simpler chemical materials that are used to construct the body parts of the adult butterfly, all of which can be accomplished in as little as two weeks. The drama inside takes place without any noticeable change in the outward appearance of the pupa. If you watch, nothing seems to be happening. In the final few days, the color and pattern of the adult's wings gradually become visible through the pupa's transparent covering.

Form 4: Adult

The long delicate legs, antennae, and wings of the butterfly are folded and compressed together within the pupal shell. At the appropriate moment, the shell splits along fault lines and the butterfly begins to push itself out. Once again, this individual is stepping out of confinement into the open world. (Does the butterfly have any recollection of emerging as a caterpillar from the eggshell? Back then, there were new legs to get the feel of, serviceable, sturdy ones, not like these long, wonderfully agile extremities. And these wings!)

The wings are soft and compliant only for a brief period. The butterfly suspends itself so its wings can hang down and straighten, using its pupal case or some other handy foothold. Body fluid is forced into the hollow veins of the wings. The wings begin to stiffen within minutes and are ready for use in an hour or so.

The principal role of the adult male butterfly is to locate a mate. The role of the female is to disperse her eggs. The adult butterfly's mobility is well matched to each role. The very first flight is tentative and comparatively awkward, but that's about as long as it takes the butterfly to learn to use its new wings.

SURVIVAL STRATEGIES ▰▰▰▰▰▰

Diapause: Escaping the Adverse Seasons

I know a mountain meadow where I can walk on a summer day and count on being entertained by butterflies rising up from flowers along the path. If I stop to hunt, I'll find caterpillars each summer on the same familiar plants. In the winter, that mountain meadow is covered with snow, and I won't see any butterflies. At another place in a desert where wildflowers cover the sandy ground in May, the resident Checkerspots and Whites flit about among the flowers. By July, warmth has turned to heat, the desert flowers are dried up, and the butterflies gone.

Most butterflies are provincial. They and their progeny live out their entire lives in one place, so they need to be prepared to survive whatever hardships that place presents, the most difficult times no less than the easy ones. When summer ends, only a few of our Northwest species, most notably the Monarch, migrate to escape the coming cold winter season. All the rest remain at their home base and adapt to the varied conditions throughout the year. They do this by entering into a state of dormancy called diapause, in which they ignore their temporarily inhospitable surroundings.

In diapause, the butterflies' metabolism is geared down to barely maintain life. Physical activity stops and any further progression of the life cycle is suspended. In any stage of development, the butterfly can initiate this half-sleep state. By conserving energy, the butterfly can stay alive in this state for many months, as a pupa even for years, without any food.

When I walk across the snow with my face stinging from the cold, the summer butterflies are all there, unseen by me. The Anglewing that flew among the asters last October has slipped from sight into a fissure in the bark of that Douglas fir, where it grabs hold and waits and waits. Eggs fastened to twigs won't hatch until spring. Tiny, young Fritillary caterpillars have crawled into the ground litter, now deeply blanketed by snow, where they will sleep until violets begin to grow again. Swallowtail pupae have postponed their transformation into adults, suspended until the change in seasons starts the necessary hormonal sequence back in motion.

Diapause is sometimes initiated at the discretion of a single individual. For example, a caterpillar may become dormant in response to its food supply drying up before it is fully grown. In other cases, diapause is incorporated as a routine part of the life cycle. For example, the caterpillars of the Checkerspot butterfly that inhabit the desert grow for a brief period in the spring, then diapause until fresh Indian paintbrush leaves reappear the following year. That's a long time to fast, but diapause occurs even in the unusually wet years when the paintbrush plants continue to offer satisfactory foliage into the summer.

The progression of metamorphosis is integrated with the seasons of the year. The timing differs between different species—for example, they may hibernate as egg, caterpillar, pupa, or adult, but all members of a given species adhere to the same plan. Adults emerge together when they can find mates; caterpillars emerge when they can expect fresh vegetation. If you discover caterpillars, you're not likely to also see adults of that species there on the same day. Conversely, if adults are flying, chances are you won't find their caterpillars.

Some butterflies have one brood per year, others have two broods, and a few have three. On the other extreme, arctic/alpine butterfly species can take more than one year to complete a life cycle. Among butterflies with multiple annual broods, diapause for winter interrupts the progression of one brood, but not the other. The first brood of Anise Swallowtail pupae form in early summer and develop into adults in two to three weeks. Pupae of the second brood form at the end of summer and enter diapause, which lasts until the following spring. Some signal related to the season (daylight length, temperature, change in foliage) apparently initiates diapause in the second brood.

Some individuals will vary from the routine, perhaps providing a kind of insurance against extinction. In species that produce two broods annually, there is the unusual individual of the first brood who deviates from its siblings and enters diapause, thus avoiding any potential environmental disasters to which other members of its generation are exposed. As another example, some pupae continue diapause for multiple years, avoiding the possibility of prolonged harsh conditions.

Taking a Rest

We get to know butterflies by watching what they do out in the open when the sun shines. But what do they do at night or when it rains? On June 6, clouds were gathering for an evening storm. The low sun broke through on and off, illuminating the west side of a little hill.

A few Silver-bordered Fritillaries still on the wing at 6 p.m. began to congregate there, where the sun warmed them. Two of them settled together on a clover stem, wings folded vertically over their backs. A couple hours later, the rain was still holding off, but the sun was gone for the day. The butterflies were in the same place, still exposed. One stretched her wings slowly back and forth for a few strokes, then folded back up.

It drizzled during the night, and the next day stayed dark and showery. I didn't return to the field until the end of the day. The two butterflies had moved a few inches, and their forewings were pulled down closer to their bodies, which had the effect of shrinking their profile. One had stepped to the underside of a large clover leaf, clinging there upside down.

The third day started with weather much the same. After a final shower, at 2 p.m. the sun glared through convincingly. I hurried back and found my subjects on the same plant, sunning themselves, wings spread, moving about. They flew directly to clover blossoms, one promptly after the other, taking nectar avidly as if they were restless and hungry after being holed up for the past 48 hours. *(From field notes, 1980.)*

High Reproductive Capacity and Population Gyrations

How long does a butterfly live? The answer varies radically depending on whether you're referring to the entire life, beginning when the egg hatches, or only that portion spent as an adult. The entire life, from egg through adulthood, is one year for butterflies that produce one brood annually. If there are two broods, the life span is shorter—a few months for the summer brood, more for the brood that hibernates. Life as an adult butterfly is shorter, no more than a few weeks in the warm seasons, several months for those that hibernate as adults.

These numbers represent maximum life spans, which are rarely achieved. The average actual lives are much shorter, because most butterflies meet premature deaths. In all stages of development butterflies are victims of freezing, drowning, starvation, infection, and predation.

To start with, ants and other small insects and spiders eat butterfly eggs and young caterpillars. Larger caterpillars, pupae, and adult butterflies are preyed upon not only by ants, hornets, ambush bugs, and spiders, but also by lizards, birds, and mice. Many parasitic flies and wasps infest caterpillars with their own eggs. Larvae hatching from these eggs burrow into the caterpillar to feed on its body, growing at the expense of the host, which ultimately dies.

As they land to feed, adult butterflies are ambushed by white or yellow crab spiders and by insects, all ready to grab the butterfly and pierce its body to suck its internal juice. Adults are pounced upon by toads, lizards, mice, and birds as they roost at night and on rainy days. Butterflies are trapped in spiderwebs—I've seen them snatched from the air by dragonflies, robber flies, and birds.

Despite these perils, butterflies obviously do manage to carry on from one generation to the next. Those few that reach maturity produce a lot of eggs, sometimes hundreds. The ability to produce a large number of eggs or offspring, referred to as high reproductive capacity, can make up for heavy subsequent losses. Also, rapid growth and short life cycles reduce their exposure to daily casualties, making it more likely that an individual will reach the finish line at the end of the gauntlet.

Some simple calculations produce a quantitative appreciation of the amount of predation and other premature death that affect the population of butterflies. Assume that one in three individuals survives each of the four stages of the life cycle: egg, caterpillar, pupa, and adult. How many starter eggs are necessary to produce a pair of reproductive parents? The answer is 170 eggs ($170 \times \frac{1}{3} \times \frac{1}{3} \times \frac{1}{3} \times \frac{1}{3} = 2$).

A crab spider ambushes a butterfly on a vetch blossom. Photo by William Neill.

Theoretically, 170 eggs would offset a mortality rate of two out of three at each stage, yielding a stable population. Now see what would happen if survival at each stage improved to two out of three. Using the same math, those 170 eggs would yield 34 reproductive adults—a population jump of 17-fold in one generation.

Animals with high reproductive capacities tend to experience rapid swings in population from one extreme to the other. When environmental conditions for survival are ideal—plentiful food or few competitors and enemies—their numbers soar. When conditions are unfavorable, the population crashes. When better times ultimately return, recovery can be swift. Butterfly populations vary quite a bit from one year to the next. Some, such as the Painted Lady and California Tortoiseshell, vary more than others.

Adaptability

In discussing reproduction, we emphasize that each individual butterfly is genetically unique. With high reproductive capacity, each new generation is a huge group of competitive, immature butterflies that represent a whole spectrum of different genetic characteristics. When the environment changes, a good chance exists that one or more of these genetic variations will be ready to capitalize. The individuals best equipped to cope with new conditions will be more likely to survive, mature and, in turn, reproduce. The composition of the new population will shift to one better suited to the changed environment.

Encountering Enemies

A Viceroy caterpillar I watched for several days had a habit of sunning on the same small willow twig. On May 3, the caterpillar was at its customary perch, under the intrusive scrutiny of my camera's zoom lens. Suddenly, a smaller ladybird beetle entered the field of vision, stage right, coming from the far end of the twig. Advancing nimbly along a narrow twig, as though balancing on a tightrope, this miniature tank looked more comic than aphid-eating predator, but then I'm not a small soft caterpillar. There was precious little room for passage, and when the beetle came into contact with the caterpillar's rear end, the caterpillar swung its head around aggressively, seeming to threaten the beetle. The beetle scampered past or over the caterpillar—it happened so fast I couldn't follow the details—and exited, stage left.

Curiously, the caterpillar kept its head thrust back in the same position with which it had confronted the beetle a moment ago. Since the position didn't seem normal, I wondered if the beetle had bitten the caterpillar during their brief encounter. In the meantime, I became distracted by other events. The following day, the caterpillar was in exactly the same position and quite dead. *(From field notes, 1980.)*

Color

The scales covering the upper and lower surfaces of a butterfly's wings are responsible for their color. Rub away the scales, and you'll see that the membranous wings underneath are transparent. The colors come mainly from pigment, although sometimes shades of blue and red are produced by refraction of light. Refraction is responsible for the shiny gloss on the upper surfaces of butterflies referred to as Blues and Coppers and for the metallic spots on the undersides of the Blues. Color produced by refraction varies depending on the angle at which one views the wings; wetting these wings makes them appear black.

Butterflies generally have extravagant coloring—most likely for mate recognition and protection against predators. To find a mate, a butterfly must be able to recognize another member of its species when it sees one. Visual clues are more obvious if the members of a species are conspicuously different from other species. The more distinctive their decorations, the easier it is for potential mates to identify each other.

Color patterns give a tactical edge in avoiding predators in several ways:

- **Camouflage:** Many butterflies blend with their background by taking on its general color tone, or by resembling something in the surroundings such as a piece of bark or a leaf (see Nevada Arctic, page 145).

- **Startle:** Bright, bold patterns, which might seem likely to attract too much undesired attention, can startle a predator when a butterfly suddenly flashes its wings as it breaks cover when disturbed. A split-second delay is all the butterfly needs to make its escape (see Two-tailed Swallowtail, page 51).

- **Decoy:** Bright markings on the hindwings of many species of Hairstreaks resemble the head of a butterfly. A bird or lizard, for example, attacks at this point, expecting to strike a fatal blow, but only tears away a bit of wing (see Gray Hairstreak, page 85). It's common to see this portion of the hindwing torn off these butterflies, evidence of a foiled predator attack.

- **Warn:** Poisonous caterpillars and adults are flamboyantly marked so predators can recognize them beforehand and avoid them (see Monarch caterpillar, page 131).

- **Mimic:** If they aren't actually dangerous themselves, some butterflies look like something that is. Several mimic other, unrelated poisonous species. If unable to distinguish the butterflies from their poisonous relatives, predators avoid both (see Viceroy, page 132).

A Swallowtail caterpillar poses as a dangerous snake (eastern U.S.). Photo by William Neill.

BUTTERFLIES AND PLANTS ▰▰▰▰

Symbiosis: Nectar Traded for Cross-fertilization

Butterflies are one of many types of insects that serve as vectors or carriers in the cross-fertilization of flowering plants.

As a butterfly probes a flower to obtain the nectar as food, its legs and body incidentally pick up pollen, which is the male element needed to fertilize a plant's ovum. Later, when the butterfly moves to another flower, some of the pollen brushes off on the flower's stigma, from where it can reach the plant's ovum or seed for fertilization. This is a mutually beneficial relationship between butterflies and plants, a phenomenon referred to as symbiosis (living together).

A plant benefits in this exchange only if the butterfly visits another flower of the same species. Otherwise, the plant achieves nothing by having its pollen deposited on some other kind of flower. It's important to remember here that animal behavior is subject to habit. A butterfly that has just received a good nectar meal at one blossom looks for another like it. Observe butterflies feeding in a field of mixed flowers—a butterfly tends to target a single species, say a white daisy, moving sequentially from one daisy blossom to the next. Eventually, this pattern is broken, only to be repeated using a different kind of flower, perhaps a yellow groundsel this time. The unique shapes and colors of flowers evolved so pollinating insects could distinguish plants in the same field. The impression, "that tasted good; where's another," induces the insect to deliver its burden of pollen to a flower of the same species. The perfect flower would provide a measured level of satisfaction to its insect diners. Too little nectar fails to attract customers, but if the butterfly's appetite is fully satiated, it will not be motivated to move on to the next blossom.

Host Plants

Nectar is nice, but plants are even more important as a source of food for caterpillars. There are two really important things to understand about butterflies: One is the life cycle and the other is the specific requirements of the caterpillar's diet. As plants were eaten by caterpillars (and other animals), they evolved procedures to defend themselves. Their defenses might be physical characteristics such as hardness or hairiness, which makes it more difficult for caterpillars to bite off pieces and digest them. Or the defense might be chemicals in their foliage that inhibit intestinal absorption or toxic substances that later kill the caterpillar if it does succeed in digesting the foliage.

Caterpillars answer the plants' challenges by devising countermeasures: perhaps enzymes to penetrate hard coatings or dissolve hairs, antidotes to toxins, or altered metabolic pathways to bypass chemical poisons. As you would expect, the caterpillar's countermeasures are usually narrowly defined to foil the defenses employed by one plant, but not necessarily those of other plants. Therefore, many caterpillars are highly specialized foragers, limited to a few related plants they can safely use as food. These are referred to as the caterpillar's host plants. It's a good term, because it places the right emphasis on the relative roles of the plants and caterpillars: the provider of a banquet and the guest. Unlike the butterfly and the flower, this is not mutually beneficial; the caterpillar gains at the plant's expense. The caterpillars refuse to eat other plants, or, if they do, they are likely to become sick or die. In this case, a butterfly can colonize only places where its host plant grows. Some caterpillars, for example the Oregon Swallowtail and Hoary Elfin, accept only one kind of a plant as food. Others, such as the Painted Lady and Gray Hairstreak, have a broader range of host plants. Caterpillars and other herbivorous insects actually help control the native plants with which they have evolved. When alien plants invade new territory, they often lack similar restraints and proliferate to become troublesome weeds.

Above: Arnica, lupine, and asters in Mt. Rainier National Park. Photo by Charles Gurche.
Overleaf: Pole fence running through a field of wildflowers at Granny Spring Viewpoint in Hells Canyon National Recreation Area, Wallowa County, Oregon. Photo by Steve Terrill.

Butterflies and You

The morning is getting on by the time the sun clears the tops of the trees behind me. The opposite edge of the meadow is hemmed in by a wall of forest. I watch the morning light march down the sides of the trees. Finally, it reaches the shrubs growing in the crease where the vertical forest and flat meadow meet. Now the warm light is chasing shadows across the meadow, melting away the dew, unveiling patches of wildflowers. Here come the butterflies, roused from their sleep in the deep grass and tangled brush. Butterflies soaring, skimming, fluttering over the flowers. The lemony Sulfurs are hogging the show, but it's the little Idas Blue that I came to see this morning.

FINDING BUTTERFLIES

Look for butterflies in the warm sunshine. You'll find them on flowers, drinking on moist ground, or on a rock or patch of bare ground that's been toasted by the sun. Find an old field, one that's been ignored by farmers and ranchers long enough to harbor a mixture of native plants. Butterflies don't stray far from the particular kind of plant their caterpillars need to eat. In many cases, a species of butterfly depends on a single kind of plant for its caterpillar—no substitutes. The plant the caterpillar uses is almost always part of the indigenous flora, not the crops and ornamentals planted by humans, so the greater the variety of native plants, the more kinds of butterflies you'll see.

Many types of flowers, native and alien, are used as sources of nectar. Butterflies favor the flowers that produce the most nectar. In the countryside, seek out dogbane, horse mint, thistle, and milkweed. It's best if the flowers are in the sun. If you don't see butterflies around these flowers, move on to another site. Chances are, there aren't many butterflies in the neighborhood. (Note that for butterflies to enjoy nectar, they need to be able to reach it. A butterfly with a short proboscis can't reach the nectar in flowers whose petals are fused into a long, tubular shape.)

Sunshine, flowers, and varied native plants are the three main elements of good butterfly habitat. So, where in the Pacific Northwest do you find this combination? The best places are:

- The open pine forests east of the crest of the Cascade Mountains, such as the headwaters of the Deschutes River or the Wenatchee Mountains.
- Riversides down in the canyons of the high, arid central plateau, such as the John Day, Owyhee, and Okanogan rivers.
- The alpine ridges and montane meadows on Mount Rainier, Mount Adams, Steens Mountain, the North Cascades, Wallowa Mountains, and Siskiyou Mountains.
- Neglected, weedy roadsides everywhere.

Butterflies follow the seasons. They're most abundant in the spring and early summer at low elevations—for example, the Columbia, Deschutes, and Illinois river canyons—and at their peak in mid and late summer in the mountain meadows of places as high as Mount Rainier, the North Cascades, and Wallowa Mountains.

Don't expect a rich assortment of butterflies in densely farmed regions. Where the fertile low prairies in western Oregon and Washington must have supported butterflies in abundance at one time, and isolated remnants still do, the original flora have been replaced by crops that are not suitable for caterpillars. The variety of butterflies in and around our population centers, for most, is also disappointing. Most caterpillars don't share our enthusiasm for exotic trees and shrubs.

GETTING UP CLOSE TO SNOOP

Butterflies are small, so satisfactory observation means getting close. Since they are wary and intent on avoiding attention, moving close enough to them calls on skill and patience. Follow these tactics to improve your chances:

- If the butterfly is flying, don't chase it. The compound eyes of insects are designed to detect movement of objects within their broad field of vision.

- A butterfly on the wing will spot your motion and keep moving farther away. It's much easier to approach a butterfly when its attention is focused on something else. If a butterfly seems interested in a flower, hang back until it has landed on the flower and begun to probe for nectar.

- Approach slowly in a line directly toward the butterfly, keeping as low a profile as possible.

- Blend your outline with a nearby shrub.

- Don't cast a moving shadow on the butterfly or where it can see it.

- Tread softly. Butterflies probably can't hear you talk, but insects detect vibrations through their legs, especially if they are on the ground.

- A butterfly drinking water from mud often remains in one place for several minutes. You may succeed in crawling to within inches, provided you proceed carefully.

- When a pair of butterflies is in the process of courting, give them space. Be patient until they have joined in copulation. Once attached, they're not likely to separate and are inclined to stay put.

Magnification also lets you get closer. Binoculars with near-focus are a big help in the field. When you're photographing butterflies using a macro lens, you may observe interesting activities while working on the focus and composition of the picture. Also, the developed film helps document the correct identification of the butterfly you were watching.

Overleaf: Balsam root and lupine meadows, Columbia Gorge, Washington. Photo by Charles Gurche.

Geography and Butterfly Habitats

The mountains of Oregon and Washington obstruct and redirect the flow of moist air coming from the Pacific Ocean, creating dramatic local differences in rainfall, temperature, flora, and fauna. The conditions for butterfly colonization differ greatly from one area to the next. The following outline describes some major features of the terrain of this region as they influence butterfly distribution. We also considered the impact of human activity on habitat and butterflies.

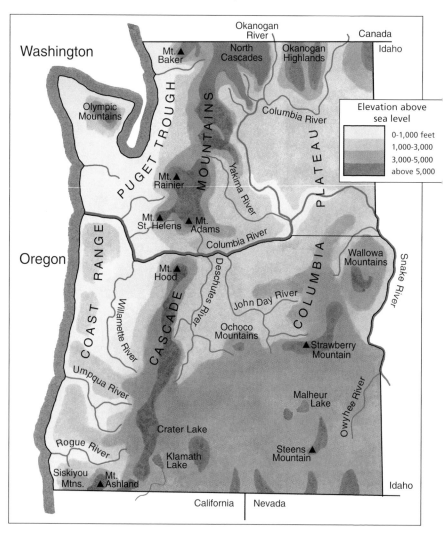

COAST RANGE

A chain of mountains, low in the center, anchored at the north end by the Olympics and at the south end by the Siskiyous.

Olympic Mountains

Highest peak: 9,000 feet
Description: wet on westward side, drier rain shadows on east side; conifer forest, subalpine meadows
Butterfly habitats: subalpine meadows, streamsides
Variety and density: medium
Examples: Gray Blue, Arctic Fritillary, Rocky Mountain Parnassian

Siskiyou Mountains

Highest peak: 7,000 feet
Description: varied local climates, some dry; open mixed conifer and deciduous forest; intrusion by California flora and fauna
Butterfly habitats: streamsides, roadsides, other forest openings
Variety and density: high
Examples: Leanira Checkerspot, Great Copper, Gray Marble, California Sister

Central Coast Range

Highest peak: 4,000 feet
Description: wet; the original forest, mostly removed by logging, has been replaced by second growth and dense brush
Butterfly habitats: streamsides, roadsides
Variety and density: low
Examples: Veined White, Satyr Anglewing, Hydaspe Fritillary

WILLAMETTE VALLEY LOWLANDS AND PUGET TROUGH

Description: flat and wet; habitats very disturbed by urbanization and farming
Butterfly habitats: edges of woods, neglected fields
Variety and density: low
Examples: Silvery Blue, Cabbage White, Purplish Copper, Sara's Orange Tip

CASCADE MOUNTAINS

Glaciated mountains with peaks reaching 10,000–14,000 feet

Western Slope

Description: 1,000–5,000 feet; wet; dense fir and hemlock forest with broadleaf evergreen understory
Butterfly habitats: forest meadows
Variety and density: low
Examples: Western Meadow Fritillary, Spring Azure, Clodius Parnassian, Pale Swallowtail

Cascade Crest

Description: 5,000–8,000 feet (butterflies scarce at higher elevations); subalpine conifer forest; montane and subalpine meadows; ridges
Butterfly habitats: montane and subalpine meadows, on rocky ridges
   Note: North Cascade portion intruded by fauna from contiguous Canadian mountains, for example, Astarte Fritillary
Variety and density: medium
Examples: Zephyr Anglewing, Western White, Northern Blue, Mariposa Copper

Eastern Slope

Description: 3,000–5,000 feet; progressively drier eastward; open pine forest with mixed shrubs and herbs under trees
Butterfly habitats: open forests, streamsides, roadsides
Variety and density: high
Examples: Pine Elfin, Nelson's Hairstreak, Lorquin's Admiral, Nevada Arctic

COLUMBIA PLATEAU

Description: 3,000–5,000 feet; flat or rolling arid prairie overgrown by sagebrush; large cultivated wheat fields
Butterfly habitats: canyons, hills
Variety and density: locally high in canyons, low on prairie
Examples: Spring White, Ruddy Copper, Two-tailed Swallowtail

Okanogan Highlands

Description: 6,000–8,000 feet; an eastward extension of the North Cascades; rolling meadows and rounded mountaintops; sparse trees
Butterfly habitats: meadows, mountaintops
Variety and density: high
Examples: Chryxus Arctic, Blue Copper, Common Alpine, Mountain Fritillary

Wallowa Mountains

Description: steep granite mountains up to 9,000 feet; forested; high lake basin, subalpine meadows, alpine ridges; faunal extensions from the Rocky Mountains
Butterfly habitats: subalpine meadows, ridges, streamsides
Variety and density: medium
Examples: Skinner's Sulfur, Milbert's Tortoiseshell, Rocky Mountain Parnassian

Ochoco Mountains

Description: 4,000–6,000 feet; rolling hills and rounded mountains; pine forest open enough to allow plentiful herbs underneath
Butterfly habitats: meadows
Variety and density: high
Examples: Western Sulfur, Callippe Fritillary, Great Spangled Fritillary, Dark Wood Nymph

Steens Mountain

Description: the west side is a prairie starting at 4,000 feet that slopes upward to a ridge at 9,000 feet; the east side is a 5,000-foot steep escarpment
Butterfly habitats: high meadows, alpine ridges
Variety and density: high
Examples: Queen Alexandra's Sulfur, Lustrous Copper, Zerene Fritillary, Shasta Blue

The eastern escarpment of Steens Mountain descends steeply from 9,000 to 4,000 feet in elevation. Photo by William Neill.

Species List

In this book, we present 100 species of butterflies found within Oregon and Washington. Most of these butterflies live in both states. Although not every species discovered in this region is included—165 different species have been reported at one time or another—the ones you are likely to encounter are presented here.

Silvery Blue. Photo by William Neill.

The 100 individual butterfly species are arranged into 15 groups based mainly on established scientific classification. We modified the organization slightly, however, by clumping together individuals that share similar physical characteristics to help in field identification. These 15 groups are organized by colored tabs in the Species Descriptions section starting on page 49.

Specialists have subdivided many of these species into two or more subspecies. Although this is useful in some cases, the status of subspecies is a fluid and often confusing subject. In the Species Descriptions section of this book, we consider each species as a single unit and make little mention of subspecies.

SWALLOWTAILS

Very large size; tail on hindwing; yellow and black.

PARNASSIANS

Large size; white with black and red spots; transparent areas of wings.

Opposite: *A male Sara's Orange Tip vividly displays his colors. Photo by Doug Hepburn.*

WHITES

Medium size; mainly white.

SULFURS

Medium size; bright yellow.

COPPERS

Small size; males iridescent on top; spotted underside.

Hairstreaks and Elfins

Small size; distinctly marked; many have hindwing tails.

Blues

Small size; males iridescent blue on top; black and sometimes orange and metallic spots on underside.

Metalmarks

Small size; dark and spotted.

FRITILLARIES

Large or medium size; top orange with black marks; spots on underside that are usually silver.

CHECKERSPOTS

Medium to small size; black, red and buff checkered pattern.

CRESCENTS

Small size; orange and ochre with black marks.

ANGLEWINGS AND RELATIVES

Medium size; irregular wing margins; dead leaf underside pattern.

ARISTOCRATS

Large size; bright colors; bold patterns.

BROWNS

Medium size; brown, orange, and gray; false eyespots.

SKIPPERS

Thick fuzzy bodies; pointed antennae; somber colors.

Leanira Checkerspot. Photo by William Neill.

Swallowtails

1 Western Tiger Swallowtail
Papilio rutulus

Doug Hepburn

Wingspan:	3⅛–3½ inches
Description:	the **top** is yellow with black vertical stripes and black wing borders. The **hindwing** has a tail, a red spot at the anal angle, and submarginal blue crescents (extensive in females).
Range:	throughout Oregon and Washington
Habitat:	forest openings and streamsides
Host plants:	varied trees, such as maple, willow, cottonwood, and aspen trees

The black stripes of the Western Tiger Swallowtail align with the long axis of its body. If you see a large yellow Swallowtail in your yard, it is probably a Western Tiger. A male is shown, replenishing himself at a mock orange blooming in May along a wooded lane. The red and blue on the hindwing are mostly hidden. The butterfly's large caterpillars are green with a pair of prominent spots near the head, designed to look like menacing snake eyes.

Opposite: *Alpine meadow in Mt. Rainier National Park, Washington. Photo by Charles Gurche.*

2 Pale Swallowtail
Papilio eurymedon
(also known as Mountain Swallowtail)

Doug Hepburn

Wingspan:	2⅞–3¼ inches
Description:	the **top** is creamy white with black vertical stripes and broad, black wing borders. The **hindwing** has a tail, a red spot at the anal angle, and submarginal blue crescents.
Range:	throughout Oregon and Washington
Habitat:	forests, mountains
Host plants:	ceanothus, alder, and buckthorn

Like the Western Tiger Swallowtail (No. 1), black stripes run parallel to the Pale Swallowtail's body. This male was taking nectar from columbine blossoms and stopped to rest on a serviceberry bush overhanging the Metolius River. The morning air was cool and still. Later, when it became hot, the air smelled of pine resin. That's the time to find groups of this butterfly on the mud at the side of the river. The caterpillar is similar to the Western Tiger Swallowtail.

3 Two-tailed Swallowtail
Papilio multicaudata

Doug Hepburn

Wingspan:	3⅜–3⅞ inches
Description:	the **top** is yellow with black vertical stripes and black wing borders. The **hindwing** has two tails, a red spot at the anal angle, and submarginal blue crescents.
Range:	east of the Cascade Mountains in Oregon and Washington, and in southwestern Oregon
Habitat:	canyons, riversides
Host plant:	chokecherry

Bigger than the other Swallowtails, the Two-tailed Swallowtail has more yellow and two tails on each hindwing. This female is feeding on thistle, a favorite nectar source for Swallowtails. The symmetrical nicks in the outer margins of both forewings are the signature of a bird's beak, presumably inflicted when the butterfly's wings were clapped together in an evasive flight maneuver, which evidently succeeded.

4 Oregon Swallowtail
Papilio oregonius

Photos by William Neill

Similar to the Anise Swallowtail (No. 5), the Oregon Swallowtail is usually bigger and has more yellow, and an eccentric pupil in the red spot. This is the official Oregon state butterfly. The illustrated adult hatched from the dark pupal shell (above) an hour earlier and is getting set to fly. Look for the large, gorgeous caterpillars on tarragon in May and, if you can stand the heat, August. A mature caterpillar that is 2 inches long is illustrated. The young caterpillars are mostly black.

Wingspan:	3⅛–3⅜ inches
Description:	the **top** is yellow with black outer margins, a black basal area of the **forewing**, and black patches along the costal margin. The **hindwing** has a tail and a red spot with an eccentric black pupil at the anal angle.
Range:	Columbia Basin in Oregon and Washington east of The Dalles
Habitat:	arid canyons
Host plant:	tarragon

5 Anise Swallowtail
Papilio zelicaon

Wingspan:	2½–2¾ inches
Description:	the **top** is yellow with black outer margins, a black basal area of the **forewing**, and black patches along the costal margin. The **hindwing** has a tail, a red spot with a centered black pupil at the anal angle, and submarginal blue crescents.
Range:	throughout Oregon and Washington
Habitat:	many, including mountaintops and urban areas
Host plant:	parsley family

The Anise Swallowtail is similar to the Oregon Swallowtail (No. 4), except smaller and darker, with the black pupil centered in the red spot. These two males are sucking moisture from the ground where an old mining road crosses Pine Creek in the Elkhorn Mountains of eastern Oregon. The immature stages of the Anise Swallowtail are shown on page 22.

Doug Hepburn

6 Indra Swallowtail
Papilio indra

Doug Hepburn

William Neill

Wingspan:	2¼–2½ inches
Description:	the **top** is black with a pale yellow band and spots. The **hindwing** has a short tail, a red spot with a central black pupil at the anal angle, and submarginal blue crescents.
Range:	east of the Cascade Mountains in Oregon and Washington, and in Oregon's Siskiyou Mountains
Habitat:	canyons and mountain ridges
Host plant:	desert parsley

You can distinguish the Indra from other Swallowtails by its dark color and stubby tails. There is only one brood annually. Adults fly in the spring (and later in mountains). The caterpillar is velvety black with contrasting yellow bands.

Parnassians

7 Clodius Parnassian
Parnassius clodius

Doug Hepburn

Wingspan:	2¼–2½ inches
Description:	the **top** is pearly white, the **forewing** has transverse dark gray bars at the costal margin, and its outer half is gray and transparent. The **hindwing** has two red spots; the antennae are solid black.
Range:	throughout Oregon and Washington, except in treeless prairies
Habitat:	moist forests
Host plant:	bleeding heart

The transparent wings appear gray where the white scales are absent. As this Clodius Parnassian sips nectar from a penstemon flower, the wings are held horizontally, acting as solar collectors. The black, fuzzy, insulated body and the dark color of the adjacent portions of the wings are designed to enhance warming of the thoracic flight muscles. These butterflies fly in early summer and their flight is slow, fluttering, and straight.

8 Rocky Mountain Parnassian
Parnassius smintheus

William Neill

Wingspan:	2–2½ inches
Description:	the **top** is white; the **forewing** has two black spots along the costal margin, often accompanied by red marks. The transparent area of the **forewing** is confined to the submarginal area in males, but is much more extensive in females. The **hindwing** has two red spots; antennae are black-and-white banded.
Range:	mountains throughout Washington, and in southwestern and northeastern Oregon
Habitat:	rock outcroppings in open forests and on mountain ridges
Host plant:	sedum

Rocky Mountain Parnassian males tend to be more opaquely white than Clodius Parnassian (No. 7), but the most consistent difference between the two species is their antennae: black and white in the former, solid black in the latter. This male is basking in the sun at 7,000 feet in the North Cascades, flattening his wings against the warm, lichen-covered rock.

Whites

9 Western White
Pieris occidentalis

Doug Hepburn

Wingspan:	1⅜–1⅝ inches
Description:	the **top** is white with black marks on the **forewing** of males and all the wings of females. The **underside** has gray-green stripes along the **hindwing** veins.
Range:	throughout Oregon and Washington, except Pacific Coast
Habitat:	many
Host plant:	mustard family

In the Western White, the black marks on the upper surface are more prominent than in the Spring White (No. 10). You may have noticed white butterflies congregated at the very summit of a mountain. The Spring White is one of many species that prefers hilltops and mountain peaks for a mating location, where males can find receptive females. Competing males arrive in the mid-morning and remain on duty until the sun slants low. Females know the plan and fly uphill to mate. Afterwards, the females return to lower elevations to find the appropriate host plant for their eggs.

10 Spring White
Pieris sisymbrii

William Neill

Wingspan:	1⅜–1⅝ inches
Description:	the **top** is white with fine black marks on the **forewing** of males and all the wings of females. On the **underside** of the **hindwing**, the wing veins have fine gold lines bordered by narrow, dull green stripes.
Range:	east of the Cascade Mountains in Oregon and Washington, in Oregon's Siskiyou Mountains, and the Olympic Mountains of Washington
Habitat:	arid prairies
Host plant:	mustard family

Spring Whites, which fly among the sagebrush in early spring, can easily be confused with Western Whites (No. 9). The wings of the Spring White are less densely covered by white scales and appear dingy, and the black markings are more delicate. The black markings are more extensive in the females of both species, however, so the subtle species difference is exaggerated by a straight comparison between the male Spring White and female Western White pictured in this book.

11 Cabbage White
Pieris rapae

Doug Hepburn

Wingspan:	1½–1⅝ inches
Description:	the **top**, which is white on males and dingy white on females, has one or two black spots and a black apex of the **forewing**. The **underside** is cream or pale olive.
Range:	throughout Oregon and Washington
Habitat:	many
Host plant:	mustard family

You can usually identify the Cabbage White by its few black spots and plain, darker underside. This is almost certainly the white butterfly you see flitting about your garden. A European butterfly, it was inadvertently introduced to this continent in the 19th century. Lacking natural restraints in the new environment, it has steadily expanded its territory over most of North America, apparently to the disadvantage of our region's related indigenous species competing for the same resources. The Cabbage White prospers around intensely developed urban regions where few other butterflies are seen. Its larva's appetite for garden vegetables even has a slight economic impact. The life cycle is repeated two or three times each year, and the adults are around from early spring into fall.

12 Veined White
Pieris napi
(also known as Mustard White)

Doug Hepburn

Wingspan:	1½–1⅝ inches
Description:	the **top** is a plain, creamy white. The **underside** of the **hindwing** is yellow-ish and the veins are outlined by a subdued brown in the spring brood.
Range:	throughout Oregon and Washington, except on treeless prairies
Habitat:	forests
Host plant:	mustard family

Most Veined Whites are without markings on the upper surface. Once common across the United States, this indigenous species has been the big loser in the competition with the intruding Cabbage Whites (No. 11). As its European relative took over the open regions across the continent, the Veined White retired mainly to the seclusion of its woods. The larvae of both species feed on mustards, but it's not known whether competition for available host plants is the only reason for the Veined White's decline.

13 Becker's White
Pieris beckerii

Photos by William Neill

Wingspan:	1⅜–1⅝ inches
Description:	the **top** is white with brown or black marks on the **forewing** of males and all the wings of females. There is a square, intense, black spot at the costal margin of the **forewing**, especially in the desert populations. The **underside** of the **hindwing** has broad olive bands along the veins, interrupted by a curved central white patch.
Range:	east of the Cascade Mountains
Habitat:	arid canyons, prairies, and deserts
Host plant:	mustard family

The field mark separating this species from the Western White (No. 9) is the interruption of the green vein lines on the center of the hindwing. The illustrated butterfly is resting on sagebrush, typical of its domain, following an unsuccessful courtship. A young caterpillar is also pictured.

14 Pine White
Neophasia menapia

William Neill

The Pine White's black-outlined forewing and the black wing veins on the underside are unique among the Whites. A Pine White has a delicate demeanor—slender body, papery wings, and a hesitant flight. They fly high in the trees, males looking for receptive females and females laying eggs. The male in the photo has come down for aster nectar. Adults are out late in the summer.

Wingspan:	1½–1¾ inches
Description:	the **top** is parchment white; the **forewing** has a black costal margin and apex. The **underside** of the **hindwing** has veins outlined in black. The **hindwing** of the female has red edges.
Range:	forests throughout Oregon and Washington
Habitat:	pine forests
Host plant:	pine trees

15 Gray Marble
Anthocharis lanceolata

The hooked forewing silhouette and gray marbling are the key field marks of the Gray Marble. Mainly a California species, they also appear in May or June in the Siskiyou and Warner mountains of southern Oregon. When the sun slipped behind a cloud on a cool spring day, this butterfly landed on the ground to keep warm. The underside blends with the somber background of its arid habitat.

Wingspan:	1½–1¾ inches
Description:	the **top** is creamy white; the **forewing** has a black dot in the center and black marks at its hooked apex. The **underside** of the **hindwing** and the apex of the **forewing** have brown-gray stippling.
Range:	southwestern Oregon
Habitat:	arid hillsides and canyons
Host plant:	rock cress

16 Sara's Orange Tip
Anthocharis sara

Photo by Doug Hepburn

Wingspan:	1⅛–1½ inches
Description:	the **top** is white in males and yellow in females. Both genders have an orange patch near the **forewing** apex. The **underside** of the **hindwing** has gray-green marbling.
Range:	throughout Oregon and Washington
Habitat:	many
Host plant:	mustard family

Sara's Orange Tip is our region's only whitish butterfly with bold, orange-red wing patches that are easily visible in flight. The male pictured above displays these orange patches on the forewings. The underside is seen on page 13. This is one of the earliest butterflies to emerge in the spring. We watched a female Sara's Orange Tip pause at a small, delicate desert mustard in the Deschutes River canyon on April 10. She left a spindle-shaped orange egg attached to the stem by its tip. The mature green caterpillar has a pale longitudinal stripe that resembles the highlight of a stem, helping it blend with the plant. The pupa, formed in May, was initially green, then faded to a warm neutral color. The pupa mimics a spent leaf—to survive, it must remain unnoticed until it hatches almost a year later.

Photos by William Neill

egg

caterpillar

pupa

17 Large Marble
Euchloe ausonides
(also known as Creamy Marble)

Doug Hepburn

Wingspan:	1⅜–1⅝ inches
Description:	the **top** is creamy white (females often golden) with black marks on the **forewing** apex. The **underside** of the **hindwing** is marbled olive green.
Range:	east of the Cascade Mountains in Oregon and Washington, and in the Siskiyou Mountains of Oregon
Habitat:	prairies, sunlit forests, montane meadows
Host plants:	mustard family and rock cress

Similar to the Small Marble (No. 18), the Large Marble is bigger, yellower, and has a more narrow, delicate black mark at the costal margin of the forewing. This butterfly is keeping in touch with her surroundings—visually by her prominent eyes, chemically by her antennae, and tactilely by motion receptors in her feet, which are ready to detect a would-be predator that carelessly jiggles the blade of grass.

18 Small Marble
Euchloe hyantis
(also known as Pearly Marble)

Photos by William Neill

Wingspan:	1¼–1⅜ inches
Description:	the **top** is white with black marks on the **forewing** apex. The **underside** of the **hindwing** has green marbling.
Range:	east of the Cascade Mountains in Oregon and Washington, and in Oregon's Siskiyou Mountains
Habitat:	canyons, deserts, and hot, dry prairies
Host plant:	rock cress

Compared with the Large Marble (No. 17), this species is smaller and whiter; the black square near the costal margin is bigger and the marbling on the underside is lime green rather than olive. Also, the Small Marble occurs in more arid terrain. The green caterpillar eats the tiny leaves of rock cress, but seems to prefer the flower petals.

Sulfurs

19 Clouded Sulfur
Colias philodice

William Neill

You can identify the Clouded Sulfur by the row of dark dots on its underside and the pearly spot encircled by two fine pink lines. In this picture, a male is taking nectar from an aster blossom near Santiam Pass in early September. The solid black border at the outer margins of the top of the wings is barely visible through to the underside.

Wingspan:	1½–2 inches
Description:	on males, the **top** is yellow with a black outer border; on females, the **top** is yellow or greenish-white with a black outer border fenestrated by yellow spots. The **underside** of the **hindwing** has a central pearly spot (with a small satellite) encircled by two pinkish-brown rings, and a submarginal row of black dots.
Range:	throughout Oregon and Washington, but uncommon west of the Cascade Mountains
Habitat:	many
Host plants:	clover and legumes

20 Orange Sulfur
Colias eurytheme

William Neill

Although the wing patterns of the Clouded Sulfur (No. 19) and the Orange Sulfur are the same, you can easily tell them apart by color, except for the white females. The orange hue often shows through to the underside more than in the photographed individual. Both species are common around urban areas and farms.

Wingspan:	1¼–2 inches
Description:	on males, the **top** is bright orange with a black outer border; on females, the **top** is bright orange or greenish-white with a black outer border fenestrated by white or orange spots. The **underside** of the **hindwing** has a pearly spot (with a small satellite) encircled by two pinkish-brown rings, and a submarginal row of black dots.
Range:	throughout Oregon and Washington
Habitat:	many
Host plant:	legumes

21 Western Sulfur
Colias occidentalis

The Western Sulfur can best be distinguished from other Sulfurs by the rich yellow color on the underside of the hindwing (both genders) and the restrained black scaling on the top of females. These males are perched on mud. The reason butterflies often cluster tightly together as they drink is not clearly understood. Is it social? For better, saltier mud? For more effective surveillance against predators?

Wingspan:	1¾–1⅞ inches
Description:	on males, the **top** is yellow with a black outer border; on females, the **top** is pale yellow and the **forewing** apex is dusted with black scales. The **underside** of the **hindwing** is golden yellow with a central pearly spot sometimes encircled by a pinkish-brown ring. The wing fringes are pink.
Range:	Olympic Mountains in Washington and the Ochoco and Siskiyou Mountains in Oregon, as well as the eastern slope of the Cascade Mountains in both states
Habitat:	open forests and meadows
Host plants:	lupine and pea

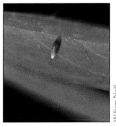

egg

22 Pink-edged Sulfur
Colias interior

William Neill

Wingspan:	1½–1¾ inches
Description:	on males, the **top** is yellow with a black outer border; on females, the **top** is yellow or pale yellow with a black outer border, which is usually on the **forewing** only. The **underside** of the **hindwing** is pale yellow with a central pearly spot sometimes encircled by a pinkish-brown ring. The wing fringes are pink.
Range:	northern Washington, east of the Cascade Mountains, northeastern Oregon, and eastern slope of the Cascade Mountains in Oregon
Habitat:	forest openings
Host plant:	blueberry

The Pink-edged Sulfur occurs across Canada and sparingly in the northern United States. This species is not easy to distinguish from the Western Sulfur (No. 21). The most useful differences are: the Pink-edged Sulfur has a pale yellow underside, it flies about two weeks later, and the females have more black on the top of their forewings. The butterfly pictured is crouched down into low foliage growing under a tamarack grove near Camp Sherman, Oregon.

23 Skinner's Sulfur
Colias pelidne

William Neill

Wingspan:	1⅜–1¾ inches
Description:	on males, the **top** is yellow with a black outer border; on females, the **top** is yellow or white and the black outer border of the **forewing** extends slightly onto the **hindwing** and is invaded by yellow or white. The **underside** is yellow suffused by black scales, especially on the **hindwing**. Wing fringes are pink.
Range:	Wallowa and Steens mountains in Oregon
Habitat:	high mountain meadows
Host plant:	blueberry

Skinner's Sulfur also resembles the Western Sulfur (No. 21), but is smaller and its underside is dusky rather than golden. Females are easier to identify by the distinctive black border, invaded at the edge in a scallop pattern. The scallop pattern does not have encircled yellow islands as in the Clouded Sulfur (No. 19) and Orange Sulfur (No. 20). Also, Western Sulfur females are seldom white. The female shown here is feeding on a composite blossom in a montane meadow. Mainly a subarctic butterfly, Skinner's Sulfur populate the high meadows of the Wallowa Mountains, where they are plentiful in August.

24 Queen Alexandra's Sulfur
Colias alexandra

William Neill

Wingspan:	1¾–2 inches
Description:	on males, the **top** is yellow with a black outer border; on females, the **top** is yellow or pale greenish-yellow and the pointed apex of the **forewing** has a black dusting. The **underside** of the **hindwing** is usually grayish-green with a small central pearly spot.
Range:	east of the Cascade Mountains
Habitat:	arid prairies
Host plant:	astragalus (locoweed)

You can usually recognize Queen Alexandra's Sulfur in the field, even from a distance. Compared to its relatives, it is larger, a more clear yellow, and found in a different habitat: arid prairies. A strong flier, Queen Alexandra's Sulfur is suited for the wide country where it lives. The male illustrated found some wet sand at the edge of a canyon stream. The caterpillars eat a bushy locoweed, astragalus, which grows on rocky arid hillsides and mountainsides. Astragalus was all over the hillside sloping down the canyon walls where this photo was taken.

Coppers

25 Lustrous Copper
Lycaena cuprea

Doug Hepburn

The Lustrous Copper is a brilliant red with black borders on the top. The forewing is yellow and the hindwing is gray on the underside. No other butterfly in our region resembles this one. Males and females are similar in this species. The Lustrous Copper looks for a habitat of meadow and adjacent open forest, usually mountainous, and it likes to visit flowers. This butterfly is not common, but isolated colonies occur in Oregon in the Ochoco, Strawberry, and Steens mountains; in the Klamath County prairie; and in the not-so-easily reached peaks of Washington's North Cascades.

Wingspan:	1–1⅛ inches
Description:	the **top** is iridescent fiery red-orange with black spots and black wing borders. The **underside** of the **forewing** is orange with white-rimmed black spots and the **hindwing** is gray with black spots and a submarginal crinkled orange line.
Range:	east of the Cascade Mountains in Oregon, and the North Cascade Mountains in Washington
Habitat:	mountain meadows
Host plant:	dock

26 Great Copper
Lycaena xanthoides

The key features of this species are the large size for a Copper, dull upper surface, and pale spotted underside. The Great Copper and Edith's Copper (No. 27) can be difficult to tell apart. The Great Copper is larger and the underside is paler and has smaller spots.

William Neill

Wingspan:	1⅛–1½ inches
Description:	the **top** is gray-brown. Females have submarginal orange crescents on the **hindwing**. The **underside** is pale buff with black spots. There are submarginal orange crescents on the **underside** of the **hindwing**, especially in females.
Range:	western Oregon
Habitat:	meadows
Host plant:	dock

27 Edith's Copper
Lycaena editha

Doug Hepburn

Like the Great Copper (No. 26), this butterfly is a conservative dresser for a Copper, and the two are easily mistaken for each other. Edith's Copper is smaller, and has large, dark-rimmed spots and a white band across the hindwing that stands out clearly against its darker underside. A common setting for Edith's Copper is a sunny meadow in the forest. The butterfly pictured is basking while it's still cool in the morning. Its knees are flexed to bring the body down close to the warm rock. Note the white band on the hindwing.

Wingspan:	1–1¼ inches
Description:	on males, the **top** is gray-brown; on females, the **top** is gray-brown streaked with dull orange, faint black spots, and faint submarginal orange crescents on the **hindwing**. The **underside** of the **forewing** is dull yellow with black spots. The **hindwing underside** is a pale gray-brown with large black-rimmed, brown spots and faint submarginal orange crescents bordered medially by an irregular white band.
Range:	the Cascade Mountains eastward in Oregon, and the southeast corner of Washington
Habitat:	mountain meadows
Host plant:	potentilla and dock

28 Ruddy Copper
Lycaena rubida

Doug Hepburn

No other Copper matches the fiercely bright red color of the male Ruddy Copper. Females are more subdued, resembling some of the other Coppers on the top. Although females are pale on the underside like the Blue Copper (No. 29), they have a warmer tan tone. Visit the arid high desert in midsummer to get a glimpse of this species. Drive the highway from John Day up past Seneca to Burns or take the road between Silver Lake and Lakeview, keeping your eye out for a red jewel on goldenrod or a metallic glint across yellow rabbitbrush.

Wingspan:	1⅛–1¼ inches
Description:	on males, the **top** is iridescent fiery red-orange; on females, the **top** is orange streaked with brown. The **underside** is cream with black spots on the **forewing** only.
Range:	east of the Cascade Mountains
Habitat:	arid prairies
Host plant:	dock

29 Blue Copper
Lycaena heteronea

Doug Hepburn

This Copper is not actually copper colored, but is blue enough to make you think it's a Blue. Older, worn males might be confused with the Common Blue (No. 48) or the Northern Blue (No. 52). The female is similar to the Ruddy Copper (No. 28), but its hue on both surfaces is cooler or bluer and the spots are often bigger. The Blue Copper likes flowers—this one is feeding on buckwheat, also the host plant of its caterpillar. Here, the wings are held vertically, but males also often alight with horizontal wings, displaying their lovely blue sheen.

Wingspan:	1⅛–1¼ inches
Description:	on males, the **top** is iridescent violet-blue; on females, the **top** is a cool slate-brown with black spots. The **underside** is ivory with black spots on the **forewing** and sometimes on the **hindwing**.
Range:	the Cascade Mountains eastward
Habitat:	mountain meadows and mountaintops
Host plant:	buckwheat

30 Purplish Copper
Lycaena helloides

Doug Hepburn

Our region's most common Copper, this is the only one that frequents the moist valleys west of the Cascades. The Purplish Copper is somewhat similar to the Lilac-bordered Copper (No. 31), but has a darker underside marked by a prominent squiggly orange line, well illustrated in the photograph. The marshy area pictured is typical habitat for this species.

Wingspan:	1–1⅛ inches
Description:	on males, the **top** is iridescent purplish-brown with submarginal orange crescents on the **hindwing**; on females, the **top** is dull orange with black spots and a black outer border. The **underside** of the **forewing** is orange with black spots and the **hindwing** is violet-brown with a submarginal orange wavy line.
Range:	throughout Oregon and Washington
Habitat:	meadows and marshy areas
Host plants:	dock and knotweed

31 Lilac-bordered Copper
Lycaena nivalis

Doug Hepburn

The bright yellow and violet Lilac-bordered Copper is easy to identify. Some, however, have a much duller underside and require a more careful look to distinguish them from the Purplish Copper (No. 30). This is a common mountain butterfly, usually in meadows near the forest and sometimes on rocky ridges above timberline. I've seen plenty of them on the Grasshopper Pass trail in the North Cascades, the ridge of Steens Mountain overlooking Kiger Gorge, and along old Route 99 at the Siskiyou summit on the way to California. The first one I ever saw was at Tombstone Prairie alongside Route 20 west of Santiam Pass. The highway sign for this historic prairie remains today, even though forest has just about swallowed the prairie. I plan to go back to see if any of the Lilac-bordered Copper colony is still holding out there.

Wingspan:	1–1⅛ inches
Description:	on males, the **top** is iridescent purplish-brown with submarginal orange crescents on the **hindwing**; on females, the **top** is dull orange with black spots and a black outer border. The **underside** is variable, but usually the **forewing** is yellow with black spots, and the **hindwing** has a yellow inner half and a violet outer half.
Range:	the Cascade Mountains eastward in Oregon and Washington, and the Olympic Mountains in Washington
Habitat:	mountain meadows and prairies
Host plant:	knotweed

32 Mariposa Copper
Lycaena mariposa

Doug Hepburn

The streaked gray hindwing of the Mariposa Copper is well illustrated in this photograph. No other Copper has this feature. Mariposa fly where blueberry thrive in open high-mountain forests. They are still on the wing, flitting among the late wildflowers, when the first snow begins to fall on the high trails.

Wingspan:	1–1⅛ inches
Description:	on males, the **top** is iridescent purplish-brown; on females, the **top** is dull orange with black spots and a black submarginal area. The **underside** of the **forewing** is yellow-orange with black spots. The **hindwing** is streaked gray with transverse rows of black wavy lines.
Range:	the Cascade Mountains eastward in Oregon and Washington, the Olympic Mountains in Washington, and the Siskiyou Mountains in Oregon.
Habitat:	mountain forests
Host plant:	blueberry

Hairstreaks and Elfins

33 Coral Hairstreak
Harkenclenus titus

William Neill

The Coral Hairstreak's row of conspicuous orange spots in the picture is distinctive. This species occurs across the northern United States, extending into the eastern portion of our region, where it is not common.

Wingspan:	⅞–1¼ inches
Description:	the **top** is a grayish-brown. The **underside** of the **hindwing** is a pale grayish-brown with a submarginal row of red-orange spots.
Range:	east of the Cascade Mountains
Habitat:	brushlands and disturbed woods
Host plants:	cherry and plum trees

34 California Hairstreak
Satyrium californica

Doug Hepburn

Wingspan:	1–1⅛ inches
Description:	the **top** is brown with an orange patch at the base of the tail. The **hindwing** has a white-tipped tail. The **underside** is light brown with a blue crescent at the base of the **hindwing** tail, the blue crescent is flanked by orange crescents, and sub-marginal rows of black and red spots.
Range:	Cascade Mountains eastward
Habitat:	brushlands and low mountains
Host plants:	oak and ceanothus

The field marks identifying the California Hairstreak are the tails and associated orange spots visible on the top and underside. These marks give the illusion of a head and are meant to induce predators to strike at a non-vital part of the butterfly.

35 Sooty Hairstreak
Satyrium fuliginosum

Doug Hepburn

Wingspan:	⅞–1⅛ inches
Description:	the **top** is a grayish brown and the **underside** is a gray-brown tweed with rows of black spots rimmed in white.
Range:	Cascade Mountains eastward in Oregon and Washington, and the Siskiyou Mountains in Oregon
Habitat:	mountain meadows and alpine areas
Host plant:	lupine

The common name Sooty Hairstreak aptly describes this drab butterfly. The gray and brown scales are mixed in a way that gives the wings a dirty or tweedy look. The only markings are indistinct spots on the underside, which can be mistaken for those of a worn Common Blue (No. 48). Take a hike above timberline at Cloud Cap to enjoy the view from Mt. Hood in midsummer, and you'll be walking past the Sooty Hairstreak on the buckwheat blossoms down by your feet.

36 Behr's Hairstreak
Satyrium behrii

Doug Hepburn

Wingspan:	⅞–1 inch
Description:	the **top** is a pale orange with wide brown borders at the costal margin and outer wing margins. The **underside** is gray-brown with white-edged angular black marks forming strong lines and triangles.
Range:	Cascade Mountains eastward
Habitat:	arid mountain foothills
Host plant:	bitterbrush

You'll recognize this species by its two-toned top and the distinctive white-edged black marks on the underside. The butterfly pictured is resting on sagebrush growing in the Behr's Hairstreak's typical hot dusty terrain, where pine forest gives way to scattered juniper and then to prairie. You'll find them along forest roads near Indian Ford campground in central Oregon and along the highway between Bend and Klamath Falls.

37 Gray Hairstreak
Strymon melinus

William Neill

Wingspan:	1–1⅛ inches
Description:	the **top** is dark gray with a black spot capped by a large orange crescent at the base of the **hindwing's** long white-tipped tail. The **underside** of the **hindwing** is pale gray with a transverse white-edged black line; there is a black spot and an orange crescent at the base of the tail.
Range:	throughout Oregon and Washington
Habitat:	many
Host plants:	legumes and many others

The orange spots adjacent to the hindwing tail are similar to those of the California Hairstreak (No. 34), but the Gray Hairstreak has much brighter orange spots and its color is gray, not brown. The butterfly pictured is making the most of his elaborate decoy pattern, keeping his real head down and out of sight. Black and white lines guide the predator's attention to the hindwing's false eyespot, which is orange with a black pupil. The long delicate tails move with the breeze and simulate antennae.

38 Green Hairstreak
Callophrys perplexa (or dumetorum)

Doug Hepburn

Wingspan:	⅞-inch
Description:	the **top** is grayish-brown on males and brown on females. The **hindwing** has a blunt tail. The **underside** is bright green with a transverse row of faint white marks.
Range:	western Oregon and Washington
Habitat:	open forests and brushlands
Host plant:	lotus

Hairstreaks with green undersides occur in many colonies in varied habitats across the Pacific Northwest. Although this type of Hairstreak surely represents more than one species, their differentiation is confusing and their nomenclature is in flux. As a group, they are easy to recognize in the field. This species, the Green Hairstreak, inhabits the lower slopes of the Cascade Mountains as well as the coastal mountains. We captured this shot at the Metolius River, where Hairstreaks deposit their pale green eggs on lotus. Often, one will dart out of the concealing foliage as you pass by. Their rapid, erratic flights are difficult to follow, but they never fly far. They always alight with the green underside on display; once spotted they are immediately recognizable.

39 Nelson's Hairstreak
Mitoura grynea
(also known as Cedar Hairstreak)

Doug Hepburn

Wingspan:	⅞–inch
Description:	the **top** is brown and the **hindwing** has a white-tipped tail. The **underside** is brownish violet, the submarginal area is bluish, and there is an incomplete transverse white line.
Range:	throughout Oregon and Washington
Habitat:	conifer forests
Host plants:	cedar and juniper

The key field marks of Nelson's Hairstreak are the tails and the beautiful violet and blue hues on the underside, seen best in bright sunlight. Adults are fond of strawberry blossoms, lomatia, and groundsel. You can find this butterfly around Memorial Day in Oregon along the Metolius River or in Washington near Lake Cushman.

40 Thicket Hairstreak
Mitoura spinetorum

Wingspan:	1–1⅛ inches
Description:	the **top** is dark blue and slightly iridescent. The **hindwing** has a white-tipped tail, and its **underside** is reddish-chocolate brown with a zigzag transverse white line, along with blue and orange marks, at the base of the tail.
Range:	Cascade Mountains eastward
Habitat:	conifer forests
Host plant:	mistletoe

Photos by Doug Hepburn

The Thicket Hairstreak's underside is marked somewhat like a Nelson's Hairstreak (No. 39), but the white transverse line is more prominent. You'll recognize the Thicket Hairstreak by the steel-blue upper surface, which is unlike any other butterfly in our area. This is a forest butterfly that occurs sparingly in scattered colonies. Occasionally, you'll see adults in the spring along forest roads, on ceanothus, or sunning on the dirt road. If you can locate mistletoe on young pine trees, you may have more luck seeing the eggs or caterpillars. The caterpillars are intriguingly well-camouflaged. The single white eggs, although small, stand out more distinctly on the mistletoe or an adjacent tree twig.

41 Pine Elfin
Incisalia eryphon

Doug Hepburn

Wingspan:	⅞–1⅛ inches
Description:	the **top** is a grayish brown on the males and brown on the females. The **hindwing** has a blunt tail and scalloped edges. The **underside** of the **hindwing** is purplish-brown with rows of angular dark lines forming sharp points. The wing fringes are black-and-white checked.
Range:	throughout Oregon and Washington
Habitat:	conifer forests
Host plant:	pine trees

The Pine Elfin is brown with a distinctive pattern of repeating triangles on the underside. This male is demonstrating typical behavior, perched on a pine bough on the lookout for a passing female. Look for these butterflies sitting on the branches of young pine—they may fly out to inspect you. The caterpillars burrow into new growth at the end of pine branches.

42 Brown Elfin
Incisalia augustinus

William Neill

Wingspan:	⅞–1 inch
Description:	the **top** is brown. The **hindwing** has a blunt tail and its **underside** has an irregular dark line separating an inner, dark brown region from an outer, paler, pinkish-brown region.
Range:	throughout Oregon and Washington
Habitat:	forests, brushlands
Host plants:	ceanothus, blueberry, and kinnikinnick

The Brown Elfin is brown with subdued markings. Last year's flower-head seems a precarious foothold for this butterfly, but it provides a panoramic view and a launching pad unobstructed in all directions. Look for this species on flowers and moist ground along roads throughout the forest.

43 Moss' Elfin
Incisalia mossii

William Neill

Wingspan:	⅞–inch
Description:	the **top** is brown. The **hindwing** has a blunt tail and its **underside** has an irregular transverse white line separating an inner, dark brown region from an outer, lighter region that contains pinkish or bluish scales. The wing fringes are white.
Range:	throughout Oregon and Washington
Habitat:	rock outcroppings
Host plant:	sedum

Although the pattern on the underside resembles that of the Brown Elfin (No. 42), Moss' Elfin has a distinct transverse white line on the hindwing and its wings are fringed with white hairs. Look for Moss' Elfin near rock outcroppings and other exposed, sunny habitats suitable for sedum. Adults emerge as early as March. In the mountains they even fly among lingering patches of snow. These butterflies usually rest on the ground, seldom visiting flowers.

44 Hoary Elfin
Incisalia polios

William Neill

Wingspan:	⅞–inch
Description:	the **top** is brown. The **hindwing** has a blunt tail; the **underside** is brown in the basal area and silvery-gray (hoary) in the submarginal area.
Range:	local colonies in coastal and northeast Oregon, and in western and northeast Washington
Habitat:	open conifer forests and brushlands
Host plant:	kinnikinnick

To distinguish the Hoary Elfin from Moss' Elfin (No. 43), look for details on the underside of the hindwing. On the former, the outer half of the wing is silvery-gray all the way to the outer margin. The latter may have pale grayish scales just beyond the white line separating the basal and outer halves of the hindwing, but the color reverts to pale brown in the submarginal area. You can find the Hoary Elfin in April near Tenino, Washington, and later in May in the pine forests between Lehman Springs and Bally Mountain in northeastern Oregon. This butterfly consistently hangs around kinnikinnick.

45 Chinquapin Hairstreak
Habrodais grunus

Doug Hepburn

Wingspan:	1⅛ inches
Description:	the **top** is golden yellow with wide brown borders. The **hindwing** has a short tail. The **underside** is a pale golden yellow with faint brown marks.
Range:	The Cascade and Siskiyou Mountains in Oregon
Habitat:	forests
Host plant:	chinquapin

You can identify the Chinquapin Hairstreak by its plain golden-yellow color. In California, the host plant is live oak; in Oregon this butterfly adapted to another *Quercus* species, chinquapin. Adults emerge in late summer. They use chinquapin flowers as a source of food, so the entire life cycle centers on the host plant. In August or September, stop along Route 26 east of Government Camp to look for this butterfly on spikes of yellow chinquapin flowers by the roadside.

Blues

46 Silvery Blue
Glaucopsyche lygdamus

Photos by Doug Hepburn

Wingspan:	⅞–1⅛ inches
Description:	on males, the **top** is bright shiny blue; on females, the **top** is suffused with black. The **underside** is pale gray with round black spots of uniform size circled by narrow white rings.
Range:	throughout Oregon and Washington
Habitat:	meadows
Host plants:	lupine and vetch

The male Silvery Blue has the brightest, shiniest top surface of any of the Blues. The iridescence results from the prismatic structure of the wing scales. The mating pair in this photograph (the browner female is on the left) demonstrate the distinctive field mark on the underside of the wings: round black spots of uniform size, each rimmed by a thin white line. This is a common meadow butterfly, at home in the mountains as well as in cultivated farmland.

Mating pair of Silvery Blues

47 Arrowhead Blue
Glaucopsyche piasus

Doug Hepburn

Wingspan:	1–1⅛ inches
Description:	the **top** is dark blue and the **underside** is gray with large black spots. The **hindwing** has white arrowheads pointed toward the body. The wing fringes are checkered.
Range:	Cascade Mountains eastward in Oregon and Washington, and the Siskiyou Mountains in Oregon
Habitat:	arid prairies and open forests
Host plant:	lupine

You can identify the Arrowhead Blue from the top by its checkered wing fringes and on the underside by the unique white arrowheads on the hindwing. It is large for a Blue and not commonly seen.

48 Common Blue
Plebejus icarioides

Doug Hepburn

Wingspan:	1–1⅛ inches
Description:	on males, the **top** is blue; on females, the **top** is suffused with black. The gray **underside** has large black spots circled by narrow white rings on the **forewing** and white spots with small black centers on the **hindwing**.
Range:	throughout Oregon and Washington
Habitat:	mountain meadows and prairies
Host plant:	lupine

To distinguish the Common Blue from the Silvery Blue (No. 46), look for the white-rimmed black spots on the underside: mainly black on the forewings, mainly white on the hindwings. Blues are fond of drinking from mud, sometimes gathering in groups on forest paths. This one found a patch of sunlight falling on a forest trail moistened by a nearby spring. They become preoccupied while drinking, so you can examine their undersides closely enough to identify one species of Blue from another. The Common Blue is widespread and numerous, especially in the mountains and high arid country east of the Cascades. A subspecies of this butterfly (Fender's Blue) has adapted specifically to Kincaid's lupine, a native plant of the Willamette Valley. As the valley was farmed and urbanized, this subspecies is now confined to the remaining small remnants of the original meadows, where Kincaid's lupine is still hanging on, but listed as an endangered species.

49 Greenish Blue
Plebejus saepiolus

Doug Hepburn

Wingspan:	⅞–1⅛ inches
Description:	on males, the **top** is greenish-blue and **underside** is bluish-gray with numerous black spots. On the females, the **top** is warm brown and the **underside** is tan with numerous black spots and faint submarginal orange spots on the **hindwing**.
Range:	throughout Oregon and Washington
Habitat:	wet meadows
Host plant:	clover

This species is consistently characterized by a greenish tint of blue in males and numerous black spots with only a trace of orange on the underside. Note the faint orange marks beneath the black triangles in the photograph. The tan underside indicates that this is a female. Her proboscis is not uncoiled for feeding; instead, her abdomen is thrust forward as if she is preparing to deposit an egg on the clover blossom, the host plant of the Greenish Blue caterpillar.

50 Acmon Blue
Plebejus acmon

Photos by Doug Hepburn

Wingspan:	¾–1 inch
Description:	the **top**, which is blue on males and brown on females, has a submarginal orange band on the **hindwing**. The **underside** is gray with black spots; the **underside** of the **hindwing** has a row of submarginal orange spots or a confluent orange band capped at the periphery by blue-green iridescent spots.
Range:	east of the Cascade Mountains and in the Olympic Mountains of Washington, and throughout Oregon
Habitat:	prairies
Host plant:	buckwheat

The Acmon Blue can be distinguished by a pattern of orange and iridescent markings. Both genders have orange spots or a band on the top and underside of the hindwing, capped on the underside with iridescent blue-green spots. The photograph demonstrates this well, although the iridescence might be more striking if viewed at a more advantageous angle of light. These butterflies are common, especially on the dry foothills that come down to the prairie. There is a second brood, so you'll spot adults at flowers and on mud from May through September.

51 Melissa Blue
Plebejus melissa

Doug Hepburn

Wingspan:	⅞–1 inch
Description:	on males, **the** top is blue; on females, the **top** is brown with a submarginal orange band on all the wings. The **underside** is gray with black spots; the **underside** of the **hindwing** has submarginal orange spots or a band capped by blue-green iridescent spots; the **underside** of the **forewing** has a few submarginal orange spots.
Range:	east of the Cascade Mountains
Habitat:	arid prairies and mountain meadows
Host plant	lupine

Orange on the underside of all wings in both genders distinguishes the Melissa Blue. Orange is repeated on top in females only. The tops of males are plain blue. This female is starting her day by warming up in the morning sun. Notice how the foliage is still fresh in midsummer in this meadow.

52 Northern Blue
Plebejus idas

Doug Hepburn

Wingspan:	⅞–1⅛ inches
Description:	on males, the **top** is blue; on females, the **top** is brown with faint submarginal orange crescents on all the wings. The **underside** is a pale, powdery gray with faint submarginal orange and iridescent blue-green spots.
Range:	high mountains throughout Oregon and Washington
Habitat:	high mountain meadows
Host plants:	lupine and legumes

The Northern Blue's design is similar to that of the Melissa Blue (No. 51), but the markings are all much fainter. Although sometimes obscure, some vestiges of orange and iridescent spots are always present. Sunlight is striking the pictured butterfly at an angle, so its underside appears darker than it really is. You can barely discern the orange spot adjacent to the black triangle on the hindwing. This is an accurate representation of how difficult it may be to see a butterfly's important field marks in typical field conditions.

53 Shasta Blue
Plebejus shasta

Doug Hepburn

Wingspan:	⅞-inch
Description:	on males, the **top** is purplish-blue; on females, the **top** is suffused with brown. The **underside** is gray with white wing veins and the **hindwing** has a submarginal row of iridescent blue-green spots capped centrally by white triangles.
Range:	east of the Cascade Mountains in Oregon
Habitat:	arid prairies and alpine mountains
Host plants:	astragalus, legumes

You can identify the Shasta Blue by the white wing veins and metallic spots accompanied by a little orange on the underside. We took this photograph at 9,000 feet on Steens Mountain, where the colony seems to be concentrated within 100 yards of the ridge overlooking the desert 5,000 feet below. To avoid being swept away by the unremitting wind, these tiny Blues restricted their flight to only a few inches above the ground.

54 Battoides Blue
Euphilotes battoides

Doug Hepburn

Wingspan:	¾–1 inch
Description:	on males, the **top** is purplish-blue, sometimes with faint submarginal orange spots on the **hindwing**; on females the **top** is brown with a submarginal orange band on the **hindwing**. The **underside** is gray with large, black, square spots on the **forewing** and a submarginal orange band on the **hindwing**.
Range:	Cascade Mountains eastward
Habitat:	arid prairies and arid mountains
Host plant:	buckwheat

While its basic pattern is similar to the Acmon Blue (No. 50), the Battoides Blue has no metallic spots. We spied several Battoides Blues congregated on coyote scat on a mountain trail, passing up the far more plentiful horse droppings strewn along the same trail. Butterflies often seek nourishment from carnivorous animal droppings or carrion. The butterfly's thin proboscis is faintly visible in this photograph. To ingest dry materials, butterflies first eject liquid through their tubes and then suck up the soup of dissolved nutrients.

55 Gray Blue
Agriades glandon

Doug Hepburn

Wingspan:	⅞-inch
Description:	on males, the **top** has a thin layer of silvery-blue scales and a row of black spots near the border of the **hindwing**; on females, the **top** is brown with pale spots showing through from the **underside**. The gray-brown **underside** has black spots encircled by white on the **forewing** and white spots and patches encircling black dots on the **hindwing**.
Range:	the Cascade and Olympic mountains
Habitat:	moist mountain meadows
Host plant:	shooting star

The Gray Blue's important field marks are on the underside: black spots, white patches, and a warm gray background. This is an alpine butterfly that flies near or above timberline, never straying far from wet meadows or depressions where its host plant, shooting star, grows. Colonies have been found in the North Cascades and Olympics in Washington and on Mount Ashland and near Crater Lake in Oregon. There must be other colonies out there awaiting discovery.

56 Spring Azure
Celastrina argiolus

Doug Hepburn

Wingspan:	⅞–1 inch
Description:	on males, the **top** is blue; on females, the **top** is partly suffused with black, especially on the **forewing** apex. The **underside** is pale gray with white streaks, small black spots, and a submarginal, irregular, fine black line.
Range:	throughout Oregon and Washington
Habitat:	open forests, varied
Host plants:	varied trees and shrubs

The pale, delicate markings and absence of any orange distinguish the Spring Azure. A male is illustrated. The Spring Azure, one of the earliest spring butterflies to emerge from its hibernating pupa, is the most common Blue in urban areas. Gregarious at water holes, crowds of these little butterflies flock to wet spots along paths through the woods all over Oregon and Washington, in April and May at low elevations and later in the mountains.

57 Western Tailed Blue
Everes amyntula

Doug Hepburn

Wingspan:	⅞–1 inch
Description:	on males, the **top** is purplish-blue; on females, the top is suffused with black. The **underside** is bluish-gray with delicate black spots. The **hindwing** has a small tail and its **underside** has a small orange and iridescent blue spot at the base of the tail.
Range:	throughout Oregon and Washington
Habitat:	forest meadows and streamsides
Host plants:	pea and vetch

This species is the only Blue with tails. The minute orange and metallic blue spot at the base of the tail helps distinguish it from the Spring Azure (No. 56) and the Silvery Blue (No. 46).

Metalmarks

58 Mormon Metalmark
Apodemia mormo

Photos by William Neill

Wingspan:	1–1¼ inches
Description:	**Top** is black with white spots and a copper patch on the **forewing**. The **underside** is streaked light gray and brown with white spots, and an orange patch is on the **forewing**. The wing fringes are checkered and the antennae are long.
Range:	east of the Cascade Mountains
Habitat:	arid prairies and canyons
Host plant:	buckwheat

The Mormon Metalmark's spotted upper surface is distinctive. It is our region's only representative of the Metalmarks, a large family of mainly tropical butterflies. Adults fly in September, when their arid surroundings lie scorched by the summer heat. The buckwheat species *Eriogonum strictum* blooms at that time in the canyons and serves as a source of nectar and as a larval host plant. Conical lavender eggs are deposited on the stems and the few remaining leaves of this and other species of buckwheat, but caterpillars do not hatch until new foliage appears the following spring.

egg

Fritillaries

59 Hydaspe Fritillary
Speyeria hydaspe

Doug Hepburn

Wingspan:	2–2¼ inches
Description:	the **top** is orange with black marks. The **underside** of the **hindwing** is purplish to maroon-brown with pale tan spots.
Range:	throughout Oregon and Washington, except on treeless prairies
Habitat:	forests
Host plant:	violet

The Hydaspe is the easiest Fritillary to identify: the underside is dark maroon and the spots are not silvered. It is the most common Fritillary in mountain forests. A good place to find them is along the roads that run through the Coast Range.

60 Great Spangled Fritillary
Speyeria cybele

Doug Hepburn

Wingspan:	2½–2¾ inches
Description:	on males, the **top** is reddish-orange (tawny) with black marks; on females, the **top** features two-toned wings divided into a dark brown basal area and a pale yellow outer area along with black marks. The **underside** of the **hindwing** is brown with a light outer band and sparse small, silver spots.
Range:	throughout Oregon and Washington
Habitat:	forests, meadows
Host plant:	violet

You can recognize males of this species by their large size, tawny color, and small silver spots. The distinctive females, with their two-toned wings, aren't apt to be confused with any other Fritillary in our territory. The Great Spangled Fritillary is widely distributed but less common than the Hydaspe Fritillary (No. 59). If you start up the footpath to Lookout Mountain in the Ochocos Mountains, you'll see the Great Spangled Fritillary, along with other Fritillaries, feeding on the mint flowers near the old mine. Keep an eye out for the unique females.

61 Zerene Fritillary
Speyeria zerene

Doug Hepburn

Butterflies are vulnerable prey during copulation. Here, this mating pair has dropped down into the seclusion of grass and weeds. The top of the male and underside of the female are visible and the tips of their abdomens are joined. The Zerene Fritillary occurs in many habitats. You can find a pale variety in the meadow near Fish Lake on Steens Mountain. A different Zerene subspecies, which is adapted specifically to the violets growing on the grassy hills overlooking the Pacific Ocean, is protected as an endangered butterfly.

Wingspan:	2⅛–2⅜ inches
Description:	the **top** is orange with black marks. The **underside** of the **hindwing** is usually tan with large silver spots.
Range:	throughout Oregon and Washington
Habitat:	forests and meadows
Host plant:	violet

62 Callippe Fritillary
Speyeria callippe

Photos by Doug Hepburn

The Callippe Fritillary's silver spots are large and elongated against the greenish background color. Males congregate in summer at the 9,000-foot summit of Strawberry Mountain and on the alpine ridges of Aneroid Mountain in the Wallowas. You can also see the Callippe Fritillary in June on the dogbane that grows along the edge of the gravel turnout at Satus Pass, Washington, or at the Simcoe Butte lookout tower nearby.

Wingspan:	2–2⅜ inches
Description:	the **top** is yellow-orange with black marks. The **underside** of the **hindwing** is pale brown, often greenish, with large elongated silver spots.
Range:	Cascade Mountains eastward
Habitat:	prairies, mountains, and alpine areas
Host plant:	violet

63 Mountain Fritillary
Speyeria mormonia
(also known as Mormon Fritillary)

Doug Hepburn

Wingspan:	1¾–1⅞ inches
Description:	orange **top** with fine black marks. The **underside** of the **hindwing** is tan with silver or pale tan spots. The wings are rounded.
Range:	Cascade Mountains eastward
Habitat:	mountain meadows and alpine areas
Host plant:	violet

Compared to others in the *Speyeria* genus, the Mountain Fritillary is smaller, brighter, and has rounded wings. These butterflies are often numerous in moist, high-mountain meadows and on peaks, where backpackers and hikers often spy them. I remember enjoying them at Louden Lake, 7,000 feet up in the Okanogan Highlands, a long day's trek from the Iron Gate trailhead. A more convenient place to see them is the Ochoco Mountains in the meadows along Marks Creek adjacent to Route 26.

64 Western Meadow Fritillary
Boloria epithore

Doug Hepburn

In our region, the Western Meadow Fritillary is the most common of the *Boloria* species. These butterflies can often be brighter than the one illustrated. Its preferred habitat is a meadow within a forest in the coastal mountains or in the foothills of the Cascades.

Wingspan:	1⅜–1⅝ inches
Description:	the **top** is orange with black marks. The **underside** of the **hindwing** has a transverse band of yellow patches in the basal area and the outer half is violet and ochre. The wings are rounded.
Range:	The Cascade Mountains to the Pacific, and sparse eastward
Habitat:	meadows
Host plant:	violet

65 Arctic Fritillary
Boloria chariclea (or titania)

William Neill

Primarily arctic, this Fritillary extends into our region in meadows just below the treeline. You can find them in midsummer on Mt. Adams, Mt. Rainier, and in the Olympics and North Cascades. This one was feeding on an aster near Harts Pass at 6,000 feet elevation. Quite variable, the Arctic Fritillary can be identified by the underside of the hindwing, which features pale angular patches on a mottled purplish background.

Wingspan:	1⅜–1⅝ inches
Description:	the **top** is orange with black marks. The **underside** of the **hindwing** is mottled purplish-brown with a transverse band of angular yellow blotches. The wing fringes are black-and-white checkered.
Range:	The Cascade and Olympic mountains in Washington
Habitat:	montane meadows
Host plant:	willow, knotweed

66 Astarte Fritillary
Boloria astarte

William Neill

Wingspan:	1⅝–1⅞ inches
Description:	the **top** is yellow-orange with black spots. The **underside** of the **hindwing** is pale orange with a transverse, irregular, buff band; the outer half of the wing is paler with a row of black dots.
Range:	the North Cascade Mountains in Washington
Habitat:	alpine areas
Host Plant:	saxifrage

A truly alpine resident, the Astarte Fritillary is at home on windswept rocky ridges in Washington's North Cascades near the Canadian border. These butterflies alight to rest reluctantly, rising up to disappear in the wind at the slightest provocation. You'll need patience to get close enough for a good look. The bare ground and lichen-covered rock in the photograph showcase its habitat. The life cycle takes two years, and adults fly only in even-numbered years.

67 Silver-bordered Fritillary
Boloria selene

Doug Hepburn

Wingspan:	1⅜–1½ inches
Description:	the **top** is bright orange with black marks and dark outer margins. The **underside** of the **hindwing** is brown and yellow with silver spots.
Range:	isolated sites in eastern Oregon and Washington
Habitat:	wet meadows
Host plant:	violet

The Silver-bordered Fritillary is the only one of the "lesser Fritillaries" (genus *Boloria*) that has silver spots. It occurs across Canada and into the Rocky Mountains of the United States. In the northwestern states, however, this species is sharply limited to a few widely scattered, tiny colonies inhabiting marshes where certain violets grow. Possibly, these colonies are ancient remnants left behind as the climate warmed. Although you can raise the caterpillars on ordinary woodland violets, the adults seem to be rigorously adapted to the wet marsh and never stray elsewhere to deposit eggs.

Checkerspots

68 Snowberry Checkerspot
Euphydryas chalcedona
(also known as Chalcedona Checkerspot)

Doug Hepburn

This the largest, darkest, and most common of all the Checkerspots. Frequently you'll spot them sitting on dirt roads through open woods, where they fly up as your car goes by. The butterfly pictured has just landed on a balsamroot flower and hasn't yet uncoiled its feeding proboscis. The topside is illustrated on page 12.

Wingspan:	1½–2 inches
Description:	the **top** is mostly black with buff spots, red wing borders, and a few red spots. The **underside** is brick red and buff. The **forewings** are long in this species.
Range:	throughout Oregon and Washington
Habitat:	open mountain slopes
Host plants:	paintbrush, snowberry, and penstemon

69 Anicia Checkerspot
Euphydryas anicia

The variety, or subspecies, of Anicia Checkerspot illustrated here flies in May and June across the sagebrush flats east of Steens Mountain. While this variety has a lot of red on top, another variety living in similar habitat not far away has virtually no red on top.

Photos by William Neill

Wingspan:	1⅜–1⅞ inches
Description:	in this variable species, the **top** is spotted black, red, and buff, while the **underside** is brick red and buff.
Range:	east of the Cascade Mountains
Habitat:	arid prairies and rock outcroppings
Host plants:	penstemon and paintbrush

70 Edith's Checkerspot
Euphydryas editha

William Neill

Wingspan:	1⅜–1⅝ inches
Description:	the **top** is spotted black, red, and buff, while the **underside** is brick red and buff. Wings are rounded.
Range:	throughout Oregon and Washington
Habitat:	mountain meadows
Host plants:	paintbrush, plantain

The rounded wings help you identify Edith's Checkerspot. The top features an overall red tone and a less sharply contrasting pattern than the other Checkerspots. If you examine the photo of the Snowberry Checkerspot (No. 68), you'll notice a whitish-buff band bordered by black lines crossing the center of the hindwing. Note that the buff color leaks past the black line, spilling to the left (peripherally) into the red area. This effect also occurs in the Anicia Checkerspot (No. 69), but not in Edith's Checkerspot, whose buff band is neatly confined by its black borders. The underside is shown on page 15. If you walk up the Iron Mountain wildflower trail in the central Cascades of Oregon, you'll see Edith's Checkerspot in July on the open rocky slope within sight of the fire tower.

71 Leanira Checkerspot
Thessalia leanira

Photos by William Neill

Wingspan:	1⅝–1¾ inches
Description:	the **top** is mainly brown with yellow spots (subspecies *oregonensis*) or mainly orange with wing veins outlined in black (subspecies *alma*). The **underside** of the **hindwing** is buff with black wing vein lines and a transverse black band containing buff spots. The body has black and buff bands.
Range:	southern Oregon
Habitat:	rocky slopes and sagebrush flats
Host plant:	paintbrush

Two subspecies of Leanira Checkerspot occur in Oregon: a dark form (*oregonensis*) in the forested Siskiyou Mountains and a light form (*alma*) in the desert basin. Shown here is the desert variety, taking nectar from a composite blossom near the edge of the barren Alvord Desert. The topside is shown on page 17. For a brief period in spring, wildflowers cover the sandy ground. Caterpillars hatch and feed on paintbrush growing in the shade of sagebrush. By June, the sun is blistering and most wildflowers wither. Young Checkerspot caterpillars begin their diapause, which lasts

through summer and winter. An older caterpillar is pictured here, out of diapause and feeding on fresh vegetation in April. The pupa blends with the dead gray sagebrush twigs. An adult will hatch from it in two weeks.

pupa   *caterpillar*

72 Northern Checkerspot
Chlosyne palla
(also known as Palla Checkerspot)

William Neill

Wingspan:	1⅜–1⅝ inches
Description:	on males, the **top** is brown and orange; on females, the **top** is dark brown with buff spots. The **underside** of the **hindwing** is dull orange with transverse bands of pale spots.
Range:	Cascade Mountains eastward
Habitat:	prairies, canyons, and open forests
Host plants:	aster, paintbrush, and rabbitbrush

This photo was taken in the lower Deschutes Canyon, where the Northern Checkerspot is common in late April and May. The males were basking on dirt or patrolling for females while both genders fed on Oregon sunshine and other flowers.

Crescents

73 Mylitta Crescent
Phyciodes mylitta

Doug Hepburn

One of our region's most common butterflies, the Mylitta Crescent occurs from sea level to high mountain meadows. Undaunted by urban sprawl, these butterflies abound around vacant lots and unattended scrubby fields, where the small black spiny caterpillars thrive on thistle. With multiple broods, adults fly from March through October. The male is well represented by this butterfly shown feeding on a daisy. The females are more heavily marked.

Wingspan:	1⅛–1⅜ inches
Description:	the **top** is orange with black marks, which are delicate in males and heavier in females. There is a broad, pale transverse band across the **forewing** and **hindwing**; the band is more conspicuous in darker females. The outer margin of the **forewing** is slightly concave. The **underside** is checkered brown, ochre, and yellow with a submarginal pale crescent on the **hindwing**.
Range:	throughout Oregon and Washington
Habitat:	many
Host plant:	thistle

74 Field Crescent
Phyciodes pratensis (or campestris)

Doug Hepburn

In males, the top side of the Field Crescent is much darker than the top side of the Mylitta Crescent (No. 73). The females of these two species are more difficult to distinguish. A clue is that the Field Crescent doesn't have angled forewings and the light and dark are more contrasting.

Wingspan:	1¼–1½ inches
Description:	the **top** is dark brown with transverse orange and ochre bands, which are more prominent in females. The **underside**, which is mostly orange on males and checkered brown and ochre on females, has a submarginal pale crescent on the **hindwing**.
Range:	throughout Oregon and Washington
Habitat:	mountain meadows and fields
Host plant:	aster

Anglewings and Relatives

75 Satyr Anglewing
Polygonia satyrus

Wingspan:	1¾–2 inches
Description:	the **top** is orange with dark brown spots and irregular outer wing margins. The **underside** is warm brown, mottled, and transversely striped (with less contrast in females). The **hindwing** has a silver comma.
Range:	throughout Oregon and Washington
Habitat:	streamsides and moist woods
Host plant:	nettle

Doug Hepburn

This is our region's only Anglewing with a warm brown underside. The picture illustrates a common basking posture with the wings held horizontally, perpendicular to the sun's rays for maximal heat absorption. The Satyr Anglewing's eggs are fastened to the underside edge of nettle leaves. Caterpillars hide on the underside of the leaves, sometimes drawing the leaves downward by silk threads in a characteristic manner. This may conceal them from predators, but can make them easier for you to locate. You can find this species anyplace where nettle grows, especially near streams in foothills of the western mountains. Around Portland, check nettle at Oaks Bottom, Portland Audubon nature trails, and Tryon State Park.

William Neill

76 Zephyr Anglewing
Polygonia zephyrus (or gracilis)

Doug Hepburn

Wingspan:	1¾–2 inches
Description:	the **top** is orange with dark brown spots and dark brown, irregular outer wing margins. The **underside** is a warm mottled gray and the outer half is lighter with vague yellowish spots. The **hindwing** has a silver comma.
Range:	Cascade Mountains eastward in Oregon and Washington, and the Olympic Mountains in Washington
Habitat:	forests and montane meadows
Host plant:	currant

While the top resembles the Satyr Anglewing's (No. 75), the underside of the Zephyr Anglewing is gray rather than brown. This photograph demonstrates the contrast between the darker inner areas and the lighter outer areas of the wings. The typical Zephyr Anglewing is actually grayer or cooler than the picture suggests. The illustrated butterfly is feeding on pearly everlasting growing at the side of a road through the Cascade forests. Zephyr Anglewings also inhabit meadows at and above timberline, where they take nectar from asters and other flowers. Look for them near the parking areas at timberline on Mount Hood and Mount Rainier.

77 Faun Anglewing
Polygonia faunus

William Neill

Wingspan:	1⅝–2 inches
Description:	the **top** is orange with dark brown spots and dark brown, irregular outer wing margins. The **hindwing** is mostly brown. The **underside** is a mottled, dark gray-brown with vague green spots. The **hindwing** has a silver comma.
Range:	western and northern Oregon, and through-out Washington
Habitat:	streamsides and moist woods
Host plants:	alder and currant

This is a small, dark Anglewing with especially ragged wing margins. The photograph shows the dark hindwing as compared to that of the Satyr Anglewing (No. 75). Sometimes the green spots on the underside of the Faun Anglewing are helpful field marks.

78 Dark Anglewing
Polygonia progne

Photos by William Neill

You can usually identify this species from other Anglewings by the uniformly dark underside. Against this background, the silver comma stands out clearly. Although uncommon, you may find the Dark Anglewing in autumn sunning on dirt roads along the Nestucca River or Mill Creek in the Oregon Coast Range.

Wingspan:	1⅞–2 inches
Description:	the orange **top** has dark brown spots and dark brown outer margins. The **hindwing** is mostly dark brown and the outer wing margins are irregular. The **underside** is mottled a very dark gray-brown (with less contrast in females). The **hindwing** has a silver comma.
Range:	western Oregon and Washington
Habitat:	streamsides and moist woods
Host plant:	currant

caterpillar

79 California Tortoiseshell
Nymphalis californica

William Neill

Wingspan:	1⅞–2⅛ inches
Description:	the **top** is orange with dark brown outer margins. A few dark brown spots dot the top of the **forewing** and one marks the **hindwing**. The wing margins are irregular and there is a small white patch near the **forewing** apex. The **underside** is mottled dark brown.
Range:	throughout Oregon and Washington
Habitat:	open forests and mountains
Host plant:	ceanothus

A close relative of Anglewings, the California Tortoiseshell can be easily mistaken for one. Generally, the California Tortoiseshell is slightly larger, not so ragged, has fewer dark spots, and has a small amount of white on the upper surface that is not present in any Anglewing. Like Anglewings, this species is fond of basking on warm earth and has a taste for nectar, as well as tree sap, carrion, and feces. Keep on the lookout for these butterflies sitting on the path ahead of you.

80 Milbert's Tortoiseshell
Nymphalis milberti

Doug Hepburn

Wingspan:	1⅝–2 inches
Description:	the **top** is brown with a bright yellow and orange transverse band. The outer wing margins are irregular. The **underside** is gray-brown and the outer half is lighter.
Range:	throughout Oregon and Washington
Habitat:	mountain meadows and streamsides
Host plant:	nettle

You'll easily recognize Milbert's Tortoiseshell by the brightly colored band across the upper side of the wings. This is one of the most common species in high mountain meadows, where it is certain to be noticed by hikers. Milbert's Tortoiseshell avidly feeds on composite flowers along trails and in meadows, pausing with wings open and colors displayed, like the one here resting on nettle. In flight it appears dark. Pale green eggs are laid in clusters on the underside of nettle leaves. Look for the spiny black caterpillars on plants with ragged, partially eaten leaves. Take a caterpillar home, feed it nettle, and you'll be rewarded with a beautiful bronze pupa. Later, you can release the adult somewhere that nettle grows.

81 Mourning Cloak
Nymphalis antiopa

Wingspan:	2⅜–2⅝ inches
Description:	the **top** is brownish-purple with bright blue submarginal spots and a cream outer margin. The outer wing margins are irregular. The **underside** is dark with a cream outer margin.
Range:	throughout Oregon and Washington
Habitat:	streamsides, forests
Host plants:	willow, aspen trees

Doug Hepburn

In our region, the Mourning Cloak is the only large dark butterfly with pale borders. The individual shown on the willow branch has emerged from hibernation. It is several months old and a little shabby. Fresher ones are a rich mahogany color with warmer cream wing margins. The adults that survive hibernation mate in the early spring. The female trusts her whole supply of eggs to one location, arranging them in a geometric mosaic encircling a willow twig. This clutch amounted to 240 eggs, most purple and a few yellow. The infant caterpillars cling together on the empty eggshells, trailing silk strands to guide them home from feeding forays. When disturbed, they snap their bodies outward in unison to create the illusion of a single formidable animal. The means of communication that makes this reaction possible is unknown. Mature caterpillars, like the one illustrated, forage alone. These spring caterpillars produce the summer brood of adults.

Photos by William Neill

eggs   *caterpillar*

Aristocrats
A Monarch, Viceroy, Admirals, Ladies, and a Sister

A fanciful, tongue-in-cheek term? The term, perhaps, but the assemblage itself is useful in field identification. These butterflies share easily recognizable physical features: they're big, bright, and bold. With the exception of the Monarch, they also are closely related to each other. Looking over the common names of the butterflies included, the collective term "Aristocrats" was irresistible to me.

82 Monarch
Danaus plexippus

Doug Hepburn

The Monarch is a transient summer resident of the Northwest. While most butterflies cope with the full cycle of seasons that comes with their breeding habitat, the Monarch flies far to the south to survive the winter. Adults that reach their destinations in Southern California (western population) or Mexico (population east of the Continental Divide) live through the winter in huge colonies. In the early spring, they begin their long return. Successive broods move northward, rearing their young on milkweed, eventually reaching Canada before the cool autumn turns them back once more. The caterpillars retain toxic alkaloids from the milkweed

Photos by William Neill

caterpillar

pupa

they eat, so the caterpillars, pupa, and adults all make birds sick when eaten. The bright, recognizable coloring of caterpillars, pupae, and adults helps remind birds of the consequences. The Monarch is common in some places, but only thinly scattered across Oregon and Washington.

Wingspan:	3½–3¾ inches
Description:	the **top** is orange with black wing veins and a black border containing white spots. The female is darker. On males, the black line in the center of the **hindwing** has an oval enlargement. The **forewing** is long and pointed.
Range:	throughout Oregon and Washington
Habitat:	open areas, including prairies and farms
Host plant:	milkweed

83 Viceroy
Limenitis archippus

William Neill

The Viceroy mimics the Monarch (No. 82). Apparently, masquerading as a king can be a profitable ploy without much attendant risk in its world. Birds avoid the perfectly digestible Viceroy, because they mistake it for a Monarch, which they know makes them sick. The Viceroy's mimicry is credited to a chance mutation that was convincing enough to birds to provide this aberrant form with enough advantage to favor survival of its offspring. The resemblance must have been refined further through survival fitness over successive generations. The Viceroy is not as large as the Monarch and has a single curved black line that crosses the other black lines on the hindwing. The Viceroy is scarce in our area, limited mainly to willow thickets along the Columbia River and its tributaries. The paucity of its look-alike in the same area may be significant—mimicry is advantageous only when the toxic species is common enough to condition the predators.

Wingspan:	2¼–2⅝ inches
Description:	the **top** is orange with black wing veins and a black border containing white spots. A curved, transverse black line crosses the veins on the **hindwing**.
Range:	east of the Cascade Mountains
Habitat:	streamsides
Host plant:	willow

84 Lorquin's Admiral
Limenitis lorquini

Doug Hepburn

Lorquin's Admiral is usually found near water, perched on vegetation, or drinking from moist ground, as this one is doing. Its flight is distinctive, with successive bursts of rapid flapping alternating with gliding, wings held out horizontally. Females place each of their eggs at the tip of a willow leaf. In the fall, a young caterpillar will roll a willow leaf into a tube, reinforce its attachment to the stem with silk, and crawl inside to swing there with the winds through the winter months. In the spring, when the new leaves come, the caterpillar pops out. The mature caterpillars, mottled brown and olive-green, are fierce-looking with warts and horns.

Wingspan:	2–2¼ inches
Description:	the **top** is very dark brown with a white transverse band and the **forewing** has an orange apex. The **underside** is similar, but lighter.
Range:	throughout Oregon and Washington
Habitat:	streamsides
Host plant:	willow

85 Red Admiral
Vanessa atalanta

William Neill

The Red Admiral's red bands and white spots are distinctive field marks. This species occurs over much of the Northern Hemisphere, but is not common in our region. The habitat is open moist woods and fields bordering woods. Unperturbed by how the evenly painted background makes him stand out as a target for bird attacks, this butterfly seems to like the vantage point on the side of a building. The Red Admiral hibernates as an adult and there is a second brood in the summer.

Wingspan:	1⅞–2⅛ inches
Description:	the **top** is very dark brown with diagonal red bands, one across the **forewing** and the other at the outer margin of the **hindwing**. The apex of the **forewing** has white spots.
Range:	throughout Oregon and Washington
Habitat:	streamsides & woods
Host plant:	nettle

86 Painted Lady
Vanessa cardui

Photos by William Neill

The Painted Lady resembles the West Coast Lady (No. 87) and the American Painted Lady (No. 88), but you can tell them apart by the white rectangular patch within the black apical area of the forewing (orange in the West Coast Lady) and the dark spots on the hindwing. The hindwings have blue centered eyespots in the other species. The Painted Lady, a cosmopolitan, worldwide butterfly, varies greatly from year to year in abundance. It does not tolerate low temperatures, so it migrates annually into the milder part of its summer range. The spiny caterpillars feed on thistle and construct loose silk nests.

Wingspan:	1⅞–2⅛ inches
Description:	the **top** is orange and black with a black area on the apex of the **forewing** that contains white spots and a white rectangle. The **top** of the **hindwing** has a submarginal row of four or five dark spots. The **underside** of the **hindwing** is mottled and has a submarginal row of 4 or 5 small eyespots.
Range:	throughout Oregon and Washington
Habitat:	open areas
Host plant:	thistle

87 West Coast Lady
Vanessa annabella

Doug Hepburn

Wingspan:	1¼–1⅞ inches
Description:	the **top** is orange and black, and the black apex of the **forewing** contains white spots and an orange rectangle. The **top** of the **hindwing** has a submarginal row of four small eyespots with blue centers. The **forewing** apex is squared. On the **underside**, the **hindwing** is mottled with a submarginal row of four or five small eyespots.
Range:	throughout Oregon and Washington
Habitat:	open areas and mountain meadows
Host plants:	nettle and mallow

You can distinguish the West Coast Lady from the Painted Lady (No. 86) by the square forewing tips, the orange (not white) rectangle within the black apical area, and the blue centered eyespots on the hindwing. Compare the photographs to see the differences. To tell the West Coast Lady apart from the American Painted Lady (No. 88), look for the square forewing tip and the row of several small eyespots on the underside of the hindwing (instead of two large eyespots). The butterfly pictured is in a basking position. This species lives in various habitats, including mountain meadows, forest openings, streamsides, and suburban gardens.

88 American Painted Lady
Vanessa virginiensis

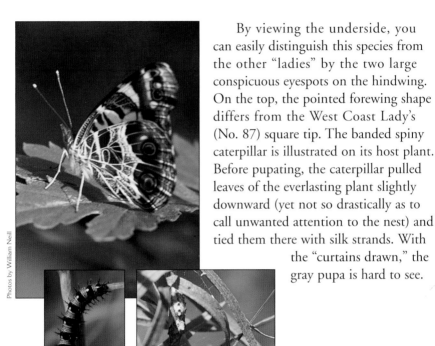

By viewing the underside, you can easily distinguish this species from the other "ladies" by the two large conspicuous eyespots on the hindwing. On the top, the pointed forewing shape differs from the West Coast Lady's (No. 87) square tip. The banded spiny caterpillar is illustrated on its host plant. Before pupating, the caterpillar pulled leaves of the everlasting plant slightly downward (yet not so drastically as to call unwanted attention to the nest) and tied them there with silk strands. With the "curtains drawn," the gray pupa is hard to see.

Photos by William Neill

caterpillar   leaves tied down to cover pupa

Wingspan:	1⅞–2⅛ inches
Description:	the **top** is orange and black, and the black apex of the **forewing** contains white spots and a white or orange rectangle. The **top** of the **hindwing** has a submarginal row of four or five small eyespots with blue centers. The outer margin of the **forewing** is concave. On the **underside**, the **hindwing** has linear streaks and two large eyespots, while the **forewing** is often pink instead of orange.
Range:	throughout Oregon, and in southern Washington
Habitat:	meadows and open weedy areas
Host plant:	pearly everlasting

89 California Sister
Adelpha bredowii

The pattern on top of the California Sister is similar to that of Lorquin's Admiral (No. 84), but the orange spot is bigger and doesn't reach the tip of the wing and the white band is narrower. The blue on the underside of the California Sister is definitive. The species is widespread in the southwestern United States, including California and the southwestern part of Oregon. The habitat is forests with oak trees. The adults fly up among the branches, but sometimes come down to drink on mud, where you can examine them more easily.

Wingspan:	2⅛–2⅝ inches
Description:	the **top** is very dark brown with a transverse white band and a large, round orange patch near the **forewing** apex. The **underside** is lighter with narrow, clear blue bands and spots around the perimeter of the wings.
Range:	western Oregon
Habitat:	deciduous forests and streamsides
Host plant:	oak

90 Buckeye
Junonia coenia

Doug Hepburn

When the Buckeye is still, you'll easily recognize it by the false eyespots on the top surface of the wings. This is a restless, pugnacious butterfly, which chases after insects and anything else that comes into view. In flight, it's a dark blur. The favorite haunt is weedy old fields crossed by dirt roads where males can sit importantly in the sun. A common butterfly in the South, the Buckeye occurs sporadically in Oregon, most often in the southwestern part.

Wingspan:	1⅝–1⅞ inches
Description:	the brown **top** has three large false eyespots. There is a buff patch on the top of the **forewing**. The **underside** is plain.
Range:	southern Oregon
Habitat:	open areas
Host plants:	plantain and others

Browns

91 Large Wood Nymph
Cercyonis pegala

Doug Hepburn

Wingspan:	1¾–2⅛ inches
Description:	**top** is brown and the **forewing** has two dark spots. The **underside** is gray-brown and finely stippled; on the **forewing**, pale yellow rings encircle two large eyespots with pale bluish pupils. Sometimes, the **underside** of the **hindwing** has eyespots.
Range:	throughout Oregon and Washington
Habitat:	open forest and prairie
Host plant:	grass

This species is very variable. In desert populations, the eyespots may be surrounded by an extensive yellow area on both surfaces of the forewing, especially in females. The camouflage pattern of this mating pair blends with the ponderosa pine bark. Larvae that hatch from the eggs will enter diapause and remain dormant until next spring, when they will awaken to begin feeding on fresh grass shoots. Adults emerge in summer.

92 Dark Wood Nymph
Cercyonis oetus

Doug Hepburn

Wingspan:	1½–1⅞ inches
Description:	the **top** is brown and the **forewing** has one or two dark spots. The **underside** is gray-brown and finely stippled. On the **underside**, the **forewing** has two eyespots with pale pupils and encircling rings, and the **hindwing** has a dark transverse zigzag line and sometimes eyespots.
Range:	the Cascade Mountains eastward
Habitat:	open forest, prairie
Host plant:	grass

This species is not always easy to distinguish from the Large Wood Nymph (No. 91). The Dark Wood Nymph is generally smaller and the best distinguishing feature is the dark transverse line on the underside of the hindwing. In the Large Wood Nymph, this line is somewhat wavy, but in the Dark Wood Nymph it is deeply zigzagged. Unfortunately, the line is hard to see in the photograph above. The background settings of the two photographs, however, give another clue to the correct identification: the mating Large Wood Nymphs are in an open forest while the Dark Wood Nymph is taking nectar from rabbitbrush growing in sagebrush prairie.

93 Ochre Ringlet
Coenonympha tullia

Doug Hepburn

Wingspan:	1–1½ inches
Description:	the **top** is ochre, a dull yellow-orange. The **underside** of the **forewing** is orange or ochre and sometimes there is an eyespot near the apex. The **underside** of the **hindwing** is gray-brown with buff marks.
Range:	throughout Oregon and Washington
Habitat:	prairies & meadows
Host plant:	grass

The Ochre Ringlet is perhaps the most numerous butterfly in Oregon and Washington. Regional variations are that east of the Cascades they often have eyespots, west of the Cascades they are plain ochre and orange (as in the photograph), and in southern Oregon they're very pale, similar to the California population. They fly low to the ground in a lazy bobbing motion, never far from the grasses upon which the green caterpillars graze. Recently, the species extended its range into New England, perhaps crossing the Canadian forests via grassy strips along new freeways.

94 Common Alpine
Erebia epipsodea
(also known as Butler's Alpine)

Doug Hepburn

The Common Alpine is found in wet meadows, usually in mountain forests, but also in open areas at lower elevations. Its flight is slow. A female is illustrated; males have less orange surrounding the eyespots.

Wingspan:	1⅛–1⅝ inches
Description:	the **top** is brown with orange patches containing several black spots, some with pupils. On the **underside**, the **forewing** is brown and the **hindwing** is grayish-brown with black spots.
Range:	east of the Cascade Mountains
Habitat:	moist meadows
Host plant:	grass

95 Chryxus Arctic
Oeneis chryxus

William Neill

Most members of this genus inhabit arctic or alpine tundra. In this cold environment, they require two years to complete their life cycles. The Chryxus Arctic occurs in the mountains of northern Washington. It rests on warm bare rocks or earth, where the stippled underside blends with the surroundings. In both our species of *Oeneis* (No. 95 and No. 96), males have specialized scent scales, used for courtship, that form a dark diagonal patch across the upper surface of the forewing.

Wingspan:	1⅞–2⅛ inches
Description:	the orange-brown **top** sports a dark outer margin, two or three eyespots on the **forewing**, and one eyespot on the **hindwing**. The **underside** of the **hindwing** is brown and white stippled with curved transverse bands.
Range:	northern Washington
Habitat:	montane meadows
Host plant:	grass

96 Nevada Arctic
Oeneis nevadensis

William Neill

Although similar to the Chryxus Arctic (No. 95), this species is larger and brighter orange, the hindwing underside is pale near its leading edge (well demonstrated in the photograph), and the outer margin of the hindwing is strongly scalloped. The two species are also separated by location: the Chryxus Arctic occurs high in mountains, while the Nevada Arctic does not live above the foothills. The Nevada Arctic is aloof and flies swiftly, so it is difficult to observe closely. It usually clings to a tree trunk or branch, then explodes in flight as it sees you approach.

Wingspan:	2–2⅜ inches
Description:	the orange-brown **top** has a dark outer margin, 2 or 3 eyespots on the **forewing**, and one eyespot on the **hindwing**. The outer wing margins are scalloped. On the **underside**, the **hindwing** is brown and white stippled with curved transverse bands.
Range:	Cascade Mountains in Oregon and Washington, and the Coast Range in Oregon
Habitat:	forest openings
Host plant:	grass

Skippers

97 Silver Spotted Skipper
Epargyreus clarus

William Neill

Wingspan:	1½–1¾ inches
Description:	the **top** is dark brown with a translucent orange patch on the middle of the **forewing**. The **underside** has an orange patch on the **forewing** and a silver-white patch on the middle of the **hindwing**. The **hind-wing** is triangular.
Range:	Oregon's Cascade Mountains westward, and throughout Washington
Habitat:	meadows and forest openings
Host plant:	legumes

You'll recognize the Silver Spotted Skipper on the wing as a dark, fast butterfly with orange and white marks. It sits on foliage and visits flowers. The forewings and hindwings are held in different planes, which makes the orange patch visible from varied angles.

98 Propertius Dusky Wing
Erynnis propertius

Doug Hepburn

The Propertius Dusky Wing has dark and somber coloring. Adults emerge as early as March, then rest on the ground, where they blend with the persisting winter litter of brown and gray sticks and leaves. Look for them at the edges of puddles with their wings spread horizontally as illustrated in the photograph.

Wingspan:	1⅜–1⅝ inches
Description:	the **top** of the **forewing** is mottled dark brown and gray. The **hindwing** is brown.
Range:	the Cascade Mountains westward
Habitat:	deciduous forests
Host plant:	oak

99 Two-banded Checkered Skipper *(Pyrgus ruralis)*

Doug Hepburn

A meadow butterfly that visits flowers, the small Two-banded Checkered Skipper is black and white. It flies in early summer and is seen in small numbers over a broad area.

Wingspan:	1–1⅛ inches
Description:	checkered wing fringes. The **top** is black with white spots
Range:	throughout Oregon and Washington, except on treeless prairies
Habitat:	mountain meadows, roadsides, and clearcuts
Host plant:	potentilla

100 Juba Skipper
Hesperia juba

Doug Hepburn

When sitting, the Juba Skipper holds its wings at an angle to the body, the forewings and hindwings in different planes. Notice how large the body is in proportion to the wings. Hold one lightly between your fingers and the strength of its flight muscles becomes apparent. The Juba Skipper is common in gardens and in arid, open countrysides throughout the region.

Wingspan:	1⅛–1⅜ inches
Description:	the **top** is gold and brown, and the body is greenish-brown. The **underside** of the **hindwing** is tan with white patches.
Range:	throughout Oregon and Washington
Habitat:	many, including meadows, prairies, and urban gardens
Host plant:	grass

Butterflies in Your Environment

The explosion of human population, prosperity, and consumption of natural resources has staggered the world's ecology. At present, it doesn't seem possible to stop human expansion. Let's consider the most important factors threatening butterflies and what realistic steps we can take on a smaller scale in our own neighborhoods.

Our contamination of the planet with toxic chemicals (an incidental by-product of our many endeavors) is harmful to animals in general, including butterflies. Moreover, we unintentionally kill a lot of butterflies when we target insects that we consider pests. Generally, the pesticides we use are toxic to a broad range of insects. Even the microbial agent Bt, which many people think infects only the gypsy moths, is in fact a germ that infects and kills the caterpillars of all butterflies and moths. Once the butterfly and moth populations have been decimated by Bt, the absence of caterpillars in the region can starve the insects, birds, and other animals that depend on caterpillars as a source of food.

The chemical and bacteriological onslaught is tough enough on butterflies, but our most significant impact on them is in shrinking and degrading the habitats where they reproduce and live. Whether through urban spread, increasing managed agricultural land, introducing invasive weeds, or tidying up any rough areas within our view, their habitat is limited or destroyed. Marshes and bogs are drained and their original plants are replaced by sprayed crops, lawns, or asphalt. Prairies are grazed and left to sagebrush or irrigated and planted with grains. Mixed forests are cut, and in their place we "reforest" with tight rows of Douglas fir. Suburbs eat up fields and woods. We are forever cutting, digging, plowing, mining, irrigating, paving, and planting. We seem bent on replacing natural diversity with an order of our own making.

We aren't likely to return many farms to native prairies, but we might be willing to manage some of the margins—brooksides, hedgerows, roadsides—in a way that is more friendly to butterflies, not to mention other native flora and fauna. The wide, sunny strips along freeways have great potential. Since they are often covered by a monoculture of some alien plant, we could try to convince the highway department to use butterfly host plants instead, many of which are attractive and hardy.

Our northwest forests are crisscrossed by dirt roads built to provide access. These roads can be an asset to butterflies—the corridors let in sunlight, and various flowers and shrubs grow along the edges of the roads. Butterflies colonize these new roadside habitats—if they are dominated by appropriate plants. Eventually, forest saplings invade and the strip is often sprayed with herbicides, or all the vegetation is cut to ground level. The life cycle of the resident butterflies is interrupted and their population crashes. These man-made corridors provide better butterfly habitats when the management style prevents encroaching forest without compromising native vegetation.

Large public landscape projects—parks, schoolyards, cemeteries, golf courses—are planted with grass and imported shrubs. Could we set aside small portions and let native plants take over?

CREATING A BUTTERFLY GARDEN

You don't have to hike or search along roadsides to find butterflies. You can create a nursery or butterfly garden and enjoy them right at home. Since success in this area depends on your ability to recognize and grow host plants, refer to the Species Descriptions section of this book for information about each species' host plants. Use the range information in the descriptions to determine if a particular butterfly is appropriate to your area.

The current enthusiasm for butterfly gardening is a hopeful sign of interest in butterfly preservation, but it isn't always focused in the best way. Gardens with flowers that provide nectar may succeed in bringing butterflies to where we can enjoy them. That has merit on its own, but what has been accomplished for butterflies? In most cases, availability of nectar is not the main factor limiting the butterfly population around our homes. Usually, residential areas are rich in flowers and poor in caterpillar host plants. Most of our landscaping, unhappily even including our butterfly gardens, can't support the life cycles of our resident butterflies. They need host plants.

In your garden, include flowers that butterflies especially like for nectar, such as bee balm, lavender, cosmos, aster, and zinnia. The flowers can be aliens if you wish. Now for the important part—be sure to place host plants nearby so female butterflies will notice them as they visit the flowers. There is a good chance they'll lay eggs on your host plants. Around Portland and Seattle, try planting thistle for Painted Lady and Mylitta Crescent, currant and nettle for Anglewings and Red Admiral, mustard for Sara's Orange Tip, and fennel for the Anise Swallowtail. Don't expect to lure butterflies that are not already residents of your general region. A butterfly that normally lives in the alpine meadows of Mount Hood or Mount Rainier is not likely to adapt to suburban Portland or Seattle, even if you do plant appropriate host plants there. Find out what butterflies live in your area, then choose the larval host plants accordingly. Of course, do not use pesticides—it's not nice to poison the guests you invite to dinner!

The place where you grow the host plants should remain rough. Leave sticks and fallen leaves in place. You'll need to tolerate enough messiness to provide a setting for the butterflies to complete their life cycle, rather than be thrown out as obscure eggs, caterpillars, and pupae along with the yard debris. The less you clean up, the better.

When creating a butterfly garden, keep these important components in mind:

- A general nectar source to bring the adults to where you can enjoy them—and where the females will notice the host plants you have set out for them.
- The specific host plants tailored to egg-laying females patrolling the neighborhood.
- A natural, undisturbed environment year-round for their life cycle.

That's what I call a butterfly garden!

MAKING A BUTTERFLY NURSERY ▮

You can watch the life cycle of a butterfly unfold in your own nursery. Raising butterflies is easy. You need only obtain an egg or caterpillar, provide the caterpillar's specific host plant, and exercise a bit of routine housekeeping.

Feeding caterpillars is not like tossing table scraps to the pet rabbit. Each species of butterfly has a specific plant that its caterpillar uses as food. Look for its eggs or caterpillars on that type of plant. Eggs are firmly attached to the foliage and they won't fall off. 'If possible, snip off the stem that holds the egg and leaf, and place the cut end in water. The foliage should be kept fresh and available for the caterpillar's first meal when it hatches a few days later. If you find a caterpillar, cage it in a roomy glass jar—a pint or quart jar will suffice. Cover the opening with cloth or netting to allow ventilation. (Note that too much ventilation dries and withers the leaves, while too little ventilation promotes mildew). Place a small amount of the host plant's leaves in the jar. Usually, the caterpillar will refuse to eat any substitute, or die if it does. Keep the jar dry, cool, and out of the sun. Empty the jar's refuse daily and replenish it with fresh leaves from the plant. Caterpillar feces are dry pellets that fall out cleanly.

The caterpillar will change to a pupa in a few weeks. Just before it does, the caterpillar stops eating, often wanders about, and may take on a sickly appearance. Don't give up hope; it is not about to die. It may eject some messy liquid, so absorbent paper at the bottom of the jar is useful. The caterpillar typically attaches itself, by silk threads, to something firm. It is apt to use the side of the jar or the cloth cover. A small twig propped up within the jar provides an alternative site and makes for easier handling of the pupa later. Once the caterpillar attaches itself in preparation for forming a pupa, do not disturb it.

The pupa itself requires no special care. It may hatch in a few weeks. Other species hibernate in this form and hatch the following spring. You can keep the jar outside over the winter—for example, a porch that is out of the rain and protected from predators is a suitable place. If the pupa is kept in a warm house, it will usually hatch earlier, before spring.

You can also obtain eggs from an adult female butterfly. To do this, enclose the butterfly together with its host plant. A cardboard box will do. If you keep an adult captive longer than a day, remove it and feed it. Soak tissue in sugar water or diluted honey, then hold the butterfly by its wings so its feet touch the tissue. Often, it's necessary to uncoil its proboscis with a toothpick to initiate feeding.

William Neill

American Painted Lady caterpillar

Surprises: If you accidentally discover an unknown caterpillar, it could be either a moth or a butterfly. A moth is more likely, since they are much more common. There is no single characteristic that separates moth caterpillars from those of butterflies. But, in general, hairless "loopers" (inchworms) and very soft, fuzzy caterpillars will turn out to be moths. Many kinds of parasitic wasps and flies lay their eggs on caterpillars, leaving no clues of their visit. If your caterpillar was infected by the time you found it, one or more of these parasites may emerge from the pupa instead of the anticipated butterfly.

THE ETHICS OF CAPTURING BUTTERFLIES

Please take a minute to think about the ethical issues surrounding catching butterflies, keeping them captive, or killing them in order to study or display them as specimens. Usually, butterflies caught in nets made of suitably soft material are not injured, but accidents occasionally do occur. Legs or wings can be broken, especially if the butterfly is caught in flight. You can significantly reduce the chance of injuring butterflies by lowering the net carefully over stationary butterflies. To hold a butterfly, it's safest to grasp it by its wings. Using your fore-finger and thumb, gently press its wings together behind its back. It doesn't hurt if you rub off a few wing scales.

Some people make collections of butterfly specimens, which entails killing them. Under almost all circumstances, taking sample specimens has no significant impact on the population nor does it pose a risk to the species. The exception is when intense, repeated collecting occurs in a population that is restricted within a small area, such as an isolated bog or mountaintop. Collectors have a responsibility to recognize and limit collecting in these vulnerable situations. In addition, collectors need to know which species are protected under the Endangered Species Act (currently, at least two subspecies in Oregon and Washington are protected).

Aside from the importance of protecting certain unique populations and species, you need to consider the morality of taking the life of any individual animal. I don't have an answer that I would attempt to impose on others. My opinion is that each of us should formulate his or her own code of ethical behavior and then be personally responsible for it. When I collect butterflies, I am restrained by the belief that every life has value. Every time I put a butterfly in my sights, I demand from myself an answer to the question: Do I want to keep this butterfly as a specimen strongly enough to be willing to take away its life?

Appendix A: Glossary

This glossary defines specialized terms used in this book in relation to butterflies.

Abdomen: The posterior (rear) segment of the body, containing digestive, reproductive, and excretory organs.

Adult: The final stage of the life cycle, when the insect possesses wings and is commonly thought of as a butterfly.

Alpine: A biological zone in the mountains above timberline, characterized by a brief summer and the low growth of specialized plants.

Anal angle: The curved margin of the hindwing near the abdomen (see diagram, page 11).

Antennae: A pair of long sensory appendages attached to the head; also known as feelers.

Apex: Tip of forewing where costal and outer margins meet (see diagram, page 11).

Arthropod: A group of animals (a phylum) characterized in particular by jointed legs and exoskeletons.

Basal area: An area of the wings adjacent to the body (see diagram, page 11).

Basking: The act of posturing in sunshine to warm the body by absorbing radiant energy from the sun.

Brood: A group of individuals of the same species that develop more or less simultaneously (in the same generation).

Caterpillar (larva): The second stage of a butterfly's life cycle, characterized by a wormlike shape with legs, eyes, and mandibles.

Chrysalis (pupa): The third stage of a butterfly's life cycle, marked by the transition between caterpillar and adult.

Copulation: The physical contact between a male and female to introduce sperm into the female's body.

Costal margin: The leading edge of the forewing (see diagram, page 11).

Cross-fertilization: The transfer of pollen between different plants of the same species.

Diapause: A dormant state in which the butterfly's activity and metabolism are greatly reduced.

Egg: The first stage of a butterfly's life cycle, starting with a fertilized ovum, then growing an embryo.

Embryo: The primitive stage of an organism's development, characterized by rapid multiplication of cells and the formation of the basic body structure.

Exoskeleton: The hard, supportive, protective outer shell of arthropods (including butterflies).

Fertilization: The combination of sperm and ovum that results in a fertilized egg.

Forewing: The pair of wings closest to the butterfly's head (see diagram, page 11).

Genus: A group of closely related species; the genus is the first word (capitalized) of the binomial scientific name of a species.

Habitat: The type of environment where a species is typically found.

Head: The anterior (front) segment of the body, containing eyes, a mouth, and antennae.

Hemolymph: The fluid inside the insect's body that surrounds its organs and is responsible for transporting nutrients and hormones.

Herb: A seed-producing plant without a permanent woody structure (for example, grasses and flowers).

Hindwing: The pair of wings furthest from the butterfly's head (see diagram, page 11).

Host plant: The species of plant that a particular species of caterpillar uses for food.

Insect: A subset (class) of arthropods that have three pairs of jointed legs.

Larva: *See caterpillar.*

Lepidoptera: A subset (order) of insects that have scales on their wings (butterflies and moths).

Life cycle: The period of growth and maturation from egg through adult butterfly.

Mandibles: Jaws for chewing.

Meadow: Land, usually somewhat moist, where grasses and herbs are the dominant plants.

Metamorphosis: The changes in physical form that occur during the life cycle (egg, caterpillar, pupa, and adult).

Montane: A biological zone in mountains below timberline, characterized by evergreen forest.

Native plant: A plant originally occupying a particular area as opposed to one that is imported.

Outer margin: The edges of the wings, away from the body (see diagram, p. 11).

Oviduct: The conduit between the exterior and the ovaries, serving as a passageway between sperm and eggs.

Ovum: The reproductive cell of the female parent, which contains half the number of chromosomes present in an adult's cell; an unfertilized egg.

Pheromone: Chemicals used for communication between courting partners.

Population: A group of individuals of the same species that occur together in the same area.

Prairie: Flat or rolling land with plants, but few or no trees (usually due to limited water).

Proboscis: The flexible feeding tube of an adult butterfly through which it sucks liquids for nourishment.

Pupa: *See chrysalis.*

Range: The broad geographic distribution of a species.

Reproductive capacity: The quantitative measure of an animal's potential for producing offspring; influenced by the number of eggs produced and the duration of the life cycle.

Species: A group of individuals that mate with each other over successive generations.

Sperm: The reproductive cell of a male parent, which contains half the number of chromosomes present in an adult's cell; it can fertilize an ovum.

Spermatophore: A packet of sperm introduced into a female during copulation.

Subalpine: A transition zone between the alpine and montane biological zones, which includes features of both.

Submarginal area: The area of the wings adjacent to the outermargins.

Subspecies: The subset of a population within a species that has its own distinctive features and is usually reproductively isolated.

Thorax: The center segment of the body where the legs and wings attach.

Treeline: The upper limit of tree growth in the mountains (also timberline).

Wing veins: The firm linear struts that reinforce the wings.

Wing fringe: Hairs at the outer margins of the wings.

Wing span: The distance between the tips of the forewings when extended horizontally with their trailing edges forming a straight line (see diagram, p. 11).

Appendix B: Bibliography

Brown, F. M., D. Eff, and B. Rotger. *Colorado Butterflies.* Denver, Colo.: Denver Museum of Natural History, 1957.

Dornfeld, Ernst. *The Butterflies of Oregon.* Forest Grove, Ore.: Timber Press, 1980. *This book is difficult to obtain.*

Ferris, C. D., and F. M. Brown. *Butterflies of the Rocky Mountain States.* Norman, Okla.: University of Oklahoma Press, 1980.

Guppy, Crispin S., and Jon H. Shepard. *Butterflies of British Columbia.* University of British Columbia Press, 2001.

Hinchliff, John. *The Distribution of the Butterflies of Oregon.* Corvallis, Ore.: Oregon State University Bookstore, 1994. *Distribution maps, no illustrations or descriptions.*

Hinchliff, John. *The Distribution of the Butterflies of Washington.* Corvallis, Ore.: Oregon State University Bookstore, 1996. *Distribution maps, no illustrations or descriptions.*

Miller, Jeffrey. *Caterpillars of Pacific Northwest Forests and Woodlands.* Washington, D.C.: Forest Service, U.S. Department of Agriculture, 1995. *Color photographs of caterpillars of butterflies and moths.*

Opler, Paul A., and Amy B. Wright. *Western Butterflies, Peterson Field Guide Series.* New York: Houghton Mifflin Co., 1999. *Covers North America west of the Great Plains and north of Mexico.*

Pyle, Robert M. *Butterflies of Cascadia.* Seattle, Wash.: Seattle Audubon Society, (due out in 2001).

Pyle, Robert M. *The Audubon Society Field Guide to North American Butterflies.* New York: Chanticler Press, 1981.

Xerces Society and Smithsonian Institution. *Butterfly Gardening.* San Francisco: Sierra Club Books, 1990.

Index

About the Author
WILLIAM NEILL

Unlike many nature writers, **William Neill** was formally trained in medicine. He grew up in the northeastern United States, where he received his undergraduate and medical training at Amherst College, Cornell Medical College, and Harvard University. For 23 years, Neill worked as a medical scientist engaged in research, teaching, and publishing in medical journals. Later, he spent six years in cardiology practice and taught at the University of Oregon Medical School from 1963 to 1976. But there is another side to William Neill—he has an enduring love for the outdoors and the natural world. Butterflies are simply a part of that love. Gradually, butterflies became the center of the outdoors for Neill. Butterfly pursuits have sent him all over the Pacific Northwest, into the Rocky Mountains, the deserts of California and Arizona, and to the arctic reaches of Alaska, Yukon Territory, and Labrador, Canada.

About the Photographer
DOUG HEPBURN

A lifelong resident of the Pacific Northwest, **Doug Hepburn** has worked as an engineer in the high-tech industry in Oregon for the last 20 years. Hepburn learned his basic photographic skills in the Navy, then followed up with classes at Portland State University. While pursuing his degree in general sciences at PSU, he took a number of classes in natural history—the love of his life. Hepburn always wanted to be a natural history photographer and dabbled in that art. While working for eight years in human genetics at the University of Oregon Health Sciences Center, he met William Neill. Once the two got to know each other, Neill proposed they combine their interests—his in butterfly collecting and Hepburn's in photography—and publish a book, *Butterflies Afield in the Pacific Northwest*. Hepburn enjoys sailing, whitewater rafting, photography, and particularly the study of the region's natural history.